QUESTIONS OF BROADCASTING

QUESTIONS
OF BROADCASTING

Stuart Hood and Garret O'Leary

Methuen

First published in Great Britain in 1990
by Methuen London
Michelin House, 81 Fulham Road, London SW3 6RB

Copyright © Stuart Hood and Garret O'Leary 1990

A CIP catalogue record for this book
is available from the British Library
ISBN 0-413-62220-7

Typeset in 10/12pt Linotron Plantin by Deltatype, Ellesmere Port
Printed in Great Britain by
St Edmundsbury Press Ltd, Bury St Edmunds
and bound by Hunter & Foulis Ltd, Edinburgh

Contents

Preface

This book developed from a project I proposed to Dr Stuart Laing, Dean of the School of Cultural and Community Studies at the University of Sussex, and which he generously supported and funded. The aim was to compile an archive of tape-recorded interviews with decision-makers in the British television industry so as to provide students interested in the role of television in society with information about how and why various decisions were made.

Between May 1988 and April 1989 I was able to conduct over fifty interviews with leading figures in the television and advertising industries. The interviews are now in the University of Sussex Broadcasting Archives. Some twenty of these interviews have been used as material for this book.

At an early stage in the project I made contact with Stuart Hood who advised me and whom I then asked to collaborate with me in putting together the book, which I am happy to say he agreed to do.

I am conscious that the book has two shortcomings. Firstly I was able to see only a limited number of people since my time and resources were limited. This meant that I was unable to interview important decision-makers outside London; secondly, at a time when many changes are taking place in the run-up to the new Broadcasting Act which will go on the Statute Book in 1990, the authors have had to meet the deadline of July 1989.

Garret O'Leary

Acknowledgments

We should like to thank Dr Stuart Laing for his support, encouragement and funding of the archive project from which this book developed. His help was crucial. We should also like to thank his assistant, Anne Woodbridge, for doing the impossible; Gillian de Jong, Peter Palmer, Bob Phillip, Lee Golding, Roger Low and Ken Whittington at the Media Service Unit at the University of Sussex for their support throughout the project; and Sue Kent for transcribing all the interviews – sometimes at very short notice. We are grateful to Richard Patterson of the British Film Institute and to Stuart Laing for reading the MS and making valuable comments. Finally, we are beholden to all those who found the time to be interviewed during a period when many of them were involved in important matters affecting the future of broadcasting in this country.

Stuart Hood
Garret O'Leary

Introduction

Broadcasting, like so many other institutions in Britain, is facing radical changes. These are partly due to technical innovations such as satellite broadcasting and the proliferation of television channels; others are the result of intervention by a government which sees people as consumers rather than as citizens and is wedded to the idea of deregulation and market forces. The changes the Government proposes are set out in a White Paper which will form the basis for legislation to be debated in Parliament in the 1989/90 session. They are far-reaching and will have profound effects on what we see and hear (and how we pay for these services) as well as on the organisation and management of the broadcasting institutions. They also call in question the concept of public service broadcasting as it has long been understood.

The proposed changes chiefly affect commercial television, which is to be deregulated and opened up to the advertisers and the market forces. They include:

1. the abolition of the Independent Broadcasting Authority (IBA), the regulatory body at present responsible for the commercial television network (ITV);
2. its replacement by an Independent Television Commission (ITC) with greatly reduced regulatory powers;
3. the setting-up of a new commercial television channel – Channel 5;
4. the requirement for Channel 4, at present subsidised by the ITV companies, to compete for its own revenue from commercial advertising; and

5. in line with the market-based approach, the proposal that the franchises to broadcast on the commercial channels – i.e. Channel 3, Channel 4, and the new Channel 5 – should be allocated by auction and must go to the highest bidder.

Where the BBC is concerned there is a strong indication that the Government wishes to see the licence fee phased out in the foreseeable future and replaced by some form of viewer subscription.

The outlines of the broadcasting debate are clear. The polarities are the ideology of the free market, on the one hand, and the concept of public service on the other. It is an important debate for many reasons: because of the immense sums of money involved; because of the implications of success or failure for a large industry, for the men and women who work in agencies, in broadcasting organisations and production companies; and because of the fact that it will decide the shape, aims and management of the most important cultural medium of our times. Its outcome will affect the way in which the majority of our fellow citizens are entertained, the extent to which they are informed and the possibilities they will have of being (directly or indirectly) educated and how much they will be expected to pay for a service they have generally felt to be 'free' and which in any terms is extremely cheap. It is a debate in which most of the contributions are lucid and are delivered with conviction; but it is impossible not to hear, in the background, at rather more than subliminal pitch, the high note of axes being ground; which is perfectly natural and understandable.

The questions being debated are not difficult to detail. Is broadcasting essentially an adjunct to the advertising industry, the main purpose of which is to deliver to the advertisers viewers, who may be part of a mass audience or members of smaller specialised audiences? Are the programmes merely bait to attract viewers who will then see the commercials? – which does not mean that the bait has to be disagreeable. Is the value of a particular audience to be measured in terms of its purchasing power? Are we, as viewers, merely targets to be sold goods, services, a life-style? Is Signor Berlusconi, the Italian television magnate, right when he says that the only criterion applicable to commercial television is profitability?

On the other side of the debate are those who take the view that children, for example, constitute a 'valuable audience' not merely because, as Sky Television's publicity puts it, 'over recent years, children's disposable income has risen dramatically'. This audience, they will argue, is a valuable one because it is composed of young people who can be stimulated, informed and entertained – even invited to think about the nature of the society and the world into which they have been born. Theirs is a point of view which does not exclude the use of the media for advertising but maintains that they also have an important social function which ought not to be lost sight of.

> It was public debate in the Fifties that led to a well
> regulated commercial system which tried to match the
> BBC in programme ambition. It became a service which
> put the interests of the viewer first. And that's the only
> British broadcasting policy we've got – a range of
> programmes that are entertaining, informative and
> educative. Not the same in America – their system is
> designed to sell goods; it's there for advertisers to use, to
> stimulate the economy and sell goods. And in other
> places it's an instrument of the state. We have in the past
> been independent of both government and to a large
> extent advertisers. A system which makes broadcasting
> more dependent than it has been on advertisers and the
> market-place is a worse broadcasting system and not a
> better one.

Television, seen from this perspective – which is that of David Plowright, the Chairman of Granada Television's Broadcasting Division – is more than a mere pastime; although it has a legitimate part to play as an aid to relaxation and legitimate pleasure.

> Television at its best is a fantastic stimulant to the
> imagination. When the BBC does *Bleak House* suddenly

the sales of Dickens pick up. We are a stimulus – we do open people's eyes . . . Television is a stimulus at its best. At its worst you sit there passively and let it wash over you. But there is room for that in people's lives. People do want something – after the strain and stress and pace of life today, people do want to sit back and have home entertainment. It's cheap and it's very agreeable. At the same time you can stimulate people to debate, to care about politics, to care about all kinds of issues television raises. The danger is that with a market-place – with the deregulation of broadcasting in this country – television will end up with too much of the passive kind of programming . . . What I hope for and what I shall fight for is to preserve Channel 4 as a public service. Probably, in the end, it will be the only public service broadcaster in the private sector.

This statement by Michael Grade, the chief executive of Channel 4, makes manifest the problem of deregulation. Can the unregulated market be allowed to follow its economic logic without social intervention? Do its activities not have to be tempered by regulation with an eye to the social implications of broadcasting? The question highlights the paradox of a government which is perfectly content to encourage intervention by a brand-new regulatory body, the Broadcasting Standards Council, when it comes to 'good taste and decency', but sets its face against a framework that would ensure that broadcasting performed certain valuable social functions and was required to pursue certain types of excellence.

That's the conundrum [says Bill Cotton, formerly Managing Director BBC Television] – that's the problem the Government have set themselves and I can't stand some of the backbench pleas that 'we're not a nannying government'. They're a perfectly decent nannying government when they want to be. So I don't see why they shouldn't do a bit of nannying when it comes down to one of the greatest achievements in society in this country over the past fifty years. And that is what we have – a highly civilised and highly successful broadcasting system.

It is unpopular in the present political climate in Britain to be prepared to say that regulation may be a positive force; but there are important voices like that of David Plowright to defend it.

There are two types of choice in the world of broadcasting – there's genuine choice and there's bogus choice. And what we are going to get out of this is bogus choice. We'll get more of the same. We will follow a similar pattern to America where you have three major networks each playing quiz or detective series programmes at the same time. That is more comedies, more quizzes, but it's not the same as the sort of range and quality we get now in the UK and should continue to get in the future. I'm a regulator and I believe that the commercial broadcasting system we have in this country has achieved its reputation in educational programmes, in information programmes, as well as entertainment programmes. The high standard of writing, of production, of direction, of performance, that is evident – not every day of the week – in the British commercial sector is there to a large extent because we've had a broadcasting system which has encouraged the pursuit of excellence, made some attempt at innovation, some willingness to show courage and take risks. That's because we haven't competed for the same source of funding with the BBC but it's also because we've had a regulatory body which has set down certain rules and nudged the system towards the ambition of originality.

The other side of the debate counts on a proliferation of channels to offer the viewers freedom of choice, the possibility of selection. But a proliferation of channels means that, while the global audience may remain more or less the same, there will be more discrete audiences more easily defined in terms of their interests and economic categories. This, as the Controller of Advertising at the IBA makes clear, has great advantages as far as the advertisers are concerned.

What will happen is that the audience will fragment into a number of pieces. Obviously if you have a proliferation of channels that will be of advantage to the advertisers – provided the fragments are homogeneous. That is to say that you get a certain concentration of affinities in any particular fragment of the audience, so that if you put a commercial in that bit of programming you are not wasting a tremendous amount of audience.

This is the concept of targeting audiences which can be defined in terms of their spending power according to a descending scale which begins with the As, Bs and Cs and continues down to the Ds and Es, whom a government minister has told us we must not call poor but who certainly have not much disposable income; they are therefore not a desirable audience.

Paul Bainsfair, managing director of Saatchi & Saatchi, has a somewhat rosy picture of a future in which the audience will be targeted in this way.

I think this proliferation of channels, if it is handled in the right way, will lead to a much more selective viewer . . . The audience will want much more information, prior to sitting down to watch television, about what they are going to see and they will want it targeted at them . . . You ought to be able to go and look in your TV guide and find what you want rather like you do in a bookshop or library. And that will bring about a big change, because I think people will probably end up watching more television overall but less television in long shots . . . There will be more trash but there will be more excellence. In other words it will just broaden out and there will be more of everything. So if you want to watch an endless diet of quiz shows then you will probably be able to do that . . . But if you want to spend most of your time watching brilliantly produced, brilliantly acted set pieces like *Brideshead* or programmes of that calibre then I think you will get more of that too.

Provided always that someone is prepared to find the very large

sums needed to finance programmes like *Brideshead Revisited*
and to nurse the talent required to make them. That will depend
on who has the ultimate say in the programme policy decisions,
as Bill Cotton spells out.

> In public service broadcasting you get money to make
> programmes and in commercial broadcasting you make
> programmes to get money. Now if the philosophy of
> commercial broadcasting takes root here that means that
> you will make programmes for exactly the amount of
> money that the people think they'll get back and not a
> penny more. And it won't be a question of whether it
> goes up or down or round about, you'll just be told how
> much money there is to make programmes with and that
> decision will be made by someone who will have more of
> a financial brain than a creative one. So it all depends
> who wins the ballgame . . . What I think will come out
> of it will probably be that the public will get more choice
> of many of the same things. They will certainly get the
> opportunity to buy a film channel. They'll certainly get
> the opportunity to have a sports channel. There will be a
> whole load of other peripheral activities. There will be a
> news channel – but that's very expensive and it's a
> bottomless pit. I don't think the public will be cheated
> so long as what is presently on offer roughly maintains
> the same sort of standards and as long as the government
> of the day, whoever it might be, ensures that this is
> true . . . There need to be people who really do want to
> add something to what I consider to be the art form of
> television. I mean a lot of people just think it's some wire
> out of which you can make a lot of money.

Or what the chairman of the Federal Communications Commission – the body that regulates broadcasting in the United
States – called 'nothing more than a toaster with pictures'.

That there is money there is clear – although the play of the
market forces also means that there are risks, as the Director of
the Incorporated Society of British Advertisers acknowledges.

We are confident that a whole lot of extra new channels will be able to be funded by advertising over the next few years. Of course they may not all succeed. That's the nature of a free market . . . If you don't provide something the viewers wish to see you have no chance of success. We take that for granted in the newspaper business or the magazine business or the publishing business, the food business. If you write a book nobody wants to read you don't deserve to sell it. There is no God-given right to success. It will be the same in television. It has not been that way in the past but the competitive nature of the market which will come about in the Nineties means that there's plenty of money for everybody to succeed if they get it right.

But the resultant changes, it is argued reassuringly by an executive at Ogilvy & Mather, the powerful advertising agency, will not necessarily be dramatic.

What we are going to be looking at is evolution and not revolution. A lot of people think that suddenly with the satellites up in the air and the White Paper out things are going to change overnight. They're not. It will evolve . . . I think because of the new channels and all the new opportunities the capital cost of getting on television will reduce, so I think we shall see a number of new categories (of advertising) coming on television . . . The style of advertising will change really as society changes. It's arguable whether advertising helps lead society or advertising follows society's changes. I think it's more the latter, i.e. we follow society rather than lead it. Will society change that much because we've got 20-odd channels instead of 4? I personally don't think so.

On whichever side they stand in the debate, everyone is agreed that change had to come. But it will not be without its dangers, as the Director of Television at the IBA explains.

Of course the system should change because there are going to be more channels to choose from and no one wishes to stop that happening. They [the broadcasters]

will have to sink or swim according to the view, the
opinions and choices the viewers make – the market, as it is
now called. But it doesn't seem to me that faced with that
the existing institutions need to be in effect destroyed . . .
But it does seem that the White Paper proposals are likely
to have the effect of destabilising – ITV certainly and
Channel 4, whose basis is by no means certain in terms of
government plans. In the longer term destabilising the
BBC if the licence fee is phased out. That's not going to be
in the interest of the British viewer who, over the years,
despite everybody's traditional complaint about television
and its standards, actually have come to enjoy and
appreciate the service which provides on four channels
currently a wide range of programmes which – not all but
many of which – are of good quality or very high quality.

Among the destabilising factors are the financial effects of a
proliferation of channels, which will take revenue out of the ITV
system, and the possibility that people, given that Channels 3
and 4 certainly (and probably 5 when it comes along) will be
'free', may begin to wonder – as some who only watch ITV
already have done – why they should pay the licence fee for the
BBC's services.

The effect on the BBC will be – and it will be sad if this
happens but it could – if people start saying 'We've got
all these channels, why do we need to pay £60 a year for
the BBC?' instead of saying 'You're paying a damn sight
more for subscription to get a few movies and the BBC
gives you a pretty stunning quality for your £60 a
year' . . . But it could be the mood of the country to say
'We're getting three free channels from ITV and we're
getting five from the BSB satellite, of which some will be
subscription, and some free ones and some subscription
from Sky, do we need the BBC at all? I hope it never
comes to that – but that's the only effect it can have, I
think. Obviously we are on the other side of the fence. A
weak BBC is little use to an IBA arguing to keep
standards up, because if you've not got high standards

coming from the BBC that's when things will just tumble down like snowflakes.

Such is the opinion of the Chairman of the IBA. How does the Director General of the BBC view his organisation's future?

I hope our audience reach will be very high – which is more important in a sense than audience share. Audience reach at the moment is 95 per cent of the public watching or listening to us at some point during the week – so that's fine, because it means that the principle of universality is being met. The audience share, I think, is impossible to predict. There are many who predict a very gloomy scenario for the BBC and say that competition will reduce the BBC share substantially. That, after all, has happened with other public service broadcasters – in Australia with ABC and in Canada with CBC – with a very, very low share of the audience for the public service broadcaster in the face of strong commercial competition. Now is that going to be the scenario for Britain? or is it going to be the scenario which is now suggested – that the fragmentation of audience will strengthen the BBC so that we'll finish up with an even higher share of the audience than our present one, which is 50 per cent? That is what is being suggested by some people in the commercial sector. I personally think there is nothing to be gained by predictions on this. I think that what the BBC has to do is keep its services going – make sure we keep our audience reach and the share will look after itself. I don't know which way it will go and I don't think anybody does – but everybody is talking and speculating.

This book is seen as a contribution to that debate. We have interviewed people involved in decision-making in the communications industry – in terrestrial television, in satellite broadcasting, in cable and in advertising. We have invited their views on the probable effects of the proposed restructuring which will be as important in the field of broadcasting as the parallel restructuring of the National Health Service or the legal

QUESTIONS OF BROADCASTING

profession. Only two of the interviewees are women; which is a comment on the opportunities for women in the upper echelons of the industry. The second part of the book consists of extracts from these interviews which are placed in a linking text. Among the topics discussed are:

the future shape of British broadcasting;
the concept of public service broadcasting;
the question of regulation;
the problem of finance;
the role of advertising;
the contribution of the independent producer;
the effect of the new technologies;
the impact of satellites;
the prospects for cable.

We hope the book will be accessible to a wide readership. Broadcasting is an important part of our daily lives. We spend an average of twenty-four hours or so a week in front of our sets. Radio and television are for most people their main source of information and entertainment. Television is a uniquely powerful medium which communicates with striking effectiveness and transcends the problems of literacy. We feel that it is important to set out the opinions of the men and women who decide what we see and hear and to learn how they envisage the future shape of broadcasting.

The book is not a history of British broadcasting. But a certain amount of history is necessary for two reasons: one is to show how the concept of public service broadcasting developed and how the BBC and the commercial network ITV came to form a public service duopoly operating under a set of rules which go back to the earliest days of broadcasting in the Twenties; the other is to chart the emergence of the argument for deregulation and with it the application of market forces to broadcasting.

We begin with that history.

PART ONE

ONE

A Definition

> **Broadcast.** *adj.* Of seed etc.: Scattered over
> the whole surface. Of sowing: Performed
> by this method. Also *fig.*
> **Broadcast.** *v.* 1. to scatter (seed, etc.) broad-
> cast. Also *fig.*
> 2. to disseminate (audible matter) from a
> wireless transmitting station. 1921.
>
> (OED)

The beginnings – the British Broadcasting Company

On 15 November 1922 *The Times* reported that 'broadcasting in this country officially began yesterday when news bulletins and weather reports were sent out from the London and Manchester stations of the British Broadcasting Company'. Each evening, the chairman of the company explained to *The Times*, there would be a brief synopsis of the world's news, prepared by the press agencies, and weather reports. In addition there would be concerts and perhaps 'speeches written by popular people to broadcast'. Later there might be developments 'from a business point of view'; but what these were he did not spell out. Most important of all, however, was his statement that broadcasting would be conducted solely from a social point of view. Thus in the earliest days of broadcasting we find a reference to the social responsibilities of the broadcasters.

Radio – 'wireless' as it was called – had existed and had been used by the military and shipping services since before the First World War. There were also enthusiastic pioneers, both amateur and professional, organised in Wireless Societies, who experimented with radio and talked over the air to each other. But there was no broadcasting as we know it – no stations putting out programmes for people to 'listen-in' to (as they said in those days). During the war, because it was feared that enemy agents might use radio, all transmissions except for official and military purposes were forbidden under the Defence of the Realm Act (DORA), which was not repealed until 1922 – four years after the end of hostilities. The moment transmissions were permitted again, the amateurs, who frequently built their own sets with imported parts, and often using skills learned in the services, began to transmit; so did the set-manufacturers, who wished to create a market for their wares. It was a confused situation which the Conservative Government of the day resolved by granting a licence to broadcast – in the sense of providing a programme service – to only one organisation: the British Broadcasting Company. The reason for the establishment of this monopoly was a purely pragmatic and possibly cynical one. The Government wished to have only one body to deal with and thus to be spared the invidious task of dealing with competing claims.

The British Broadcasting Company was the creation of the six largest radio manufacturers, who between them controlled the British patents on radio equipment. They had come together for mixed motives. One was to create an audience and tempt its members to buy wireless sets. Another was to discourage amateurs from building sets with parts bought from the United States or Europe and so to protect British manufacturers. In order to operate a wireless set, which was to bear the BBC trademark, a member of the public required a licence which cost ten shillings, a considerable sum in those days. Half the proceeds of the licence revenue went to the Company; the Government – that is to say, the Treasury – kept the other half. Without a licence the listener was breaking the law. The licence fee was, in fact, a tax. It was – and still is – a criminal offence not to pay it.

The political climate

Broadcasting was regarded with considerable suspicion by

politicians in the years that saw its official birth. These were turbulent times. In 1920 there was a strike in the police force. That same year the British Government passed an Emergency Powers Act to deal with the possibility of social and political unrest. The emergency powers were used during the miners' strike of 1921. Although the war had long been over it was not until 1922 that DORA was repealed. The reluctance to do away with its provisions reflected the nervousness of the Government at events not only at home and in Ireland but abroad where the Russian Revolution of 1917 had been followed by uprisings in Germany and Hungary. It cannot have escaped official notice that both the Russian and German revolutionaries – like the Irish rebels of 1916, who declared the Republic by wireless – had used radio to proclaim their aims. It was against this background that the Wireless Committee of the Imperial Communications Committee proposed that British receivers should be so constructed that they could not receive transmissions on certain wavelengths. This would prevent listeners from picking up broadcasts from foreign stations and so hearing dangerous thoughts. Politicians asked what would happen if broadcasting fell into the wrong hands. Was it not likely that communication by radio would be 'a danger to the good of the people'? That was the question posed in 1923 by powerful voices on the Right. It was symptomatic of the nervousness of politicians that when the Postmaster-General announced the Government's decision to let the British Broadcasting Company proceed one Tory MP at once cried out: 'Who is to censor it?'

Radio, therefore, from its earliest days, was seen as a powerful and potentially dangerous means of communication, which transmitted messages using invisible electromagnetic waves – signals which any Jack or Jill could pick out of the air. This placed the new medium – not that the word was yet commonly used in that sense – in a different category from the press or books, which had not been regulated by government since the attempts to muzzle the radical press at the time of the French

Revolution or later, in the 1840s, by press taxes – the 'taxes on knowledge'. It was inevitable that the authorities should wish to see it in safe hands.

The British Broadcasting Company was short-lived. Amateurs persisted in building their own sets. The smaller companies, egged on by powerful press interests which had not been able to get into radio and could rightly be accused of sour grapes, saw it as a monopoly to enrich the six large firms. It was a confused and messy situation. In an attempt to clear it up the Government in 1923 set up the first of many committees that, over the years, would look into broadcasting and prescribe how it should be managed. It concluded that the wavebands available in any country for broadcasting must be regarded as 'a valuable form of public property'. It also considered that the control of such a potential power over public opinion and the life of the nation ought to remain with the state but drew the line at direct government control. During the hearings of this committee the interventions of the British Broadcasting Company's managing director, a certain John Reith, were clear and forceful. Drawing on the Scottish Presbyterian tradition of moral earnestness and good works by which he had been formed, he was to leave a deep and lasting imprint on British broadcasting.

Reith and the concept of public service

In spoken and written pronouncements in the early Twenties Reith made clear how he thought broadcasting should be managed and how he saw its relationship to the state and to society.

Describing the way the Company functioned under his direction, he stressed the importance of monopoly and central control. These were desirable not only for efficiency and economy in operation, but also ethically in order that one general policy could be maintained throughout the country and definite standards promulgated. Station directors were allowed scope up to a point, but where anything might verge on policy it had to be referred to Head Office so that there was unity of control. The advantage of this highly centralised system was, in his opinion, that it permitted full administrative control and effective censorship.

There was, however, another side to Reith's view of the role of the Company. In stating it he began to formulate the concept of public service broadcasting. The Company was, he said, 'a public utility company', which was not out to make money. It was a friend of the people since public service was one of the essential characteristics of friendship. The Company had been licensed to exploit a great scientific invention, but to do so 'for the purpose and pursuit of entertainment alone' would have been a prostitution of its powers and an insult to the character and intelligence of the people. He had heard it argued that in so far as broadcasting was awakening interest in hitherto more or less inaccessible regions it was fraught with danger to the community and to the country in general. It followed that the maintenance of a high moral standard was of paramount importance. Few, he argued, would question the desirability of refraining from anything approaching vulgarity or directing attention to 'unsavoury subjects such as racing form and starting prices'. In another area he pointed to the need for similar caution. It had been considered wise policy, he said, for the Company to refrain from controversies as a general principle but the tendency was in the direction of greater freedom, although he hoped the Company would be very cautious indeed. (In fact he was in the habit of submitting 'potentially controversial speeches' to the Post Office, the government department responsible for broadcasting, which banned a number of them.)

As for the position of broadcasting in society, Reith agreed that a service 'fraught with such potentialities should be under the direct care of the state or a board composed of representatives of the public with no other interests at stake'. He went on to argue that, at a time when efforts were being made towards the nationalisation of certain essential industries of the country, the progress of broadcasting was the most outstanding example of the potentiality for combining private enterprise and public control.

BBC – the Corporation

In the event the private enterprise element fell away, the interests which had set up the Company were content to hand over the increasingly complicated and expensive business of providing programmes to another body while they got on with the manufacture of sets. That other body was the British Broadcasting Corporation, which was set up in 1927. Power was passed to it on the recommendation of yet another government committee which ruled that 'the broadcasting service should be conducted by a public corporation acting as a Trustee for the national interest and that its status and duties should correspond with those of a public service'. It was an outcome for which Reith had persistently lobbied. The Corporation, of which he inevitably became the first Director General, was set up under a royal charter which had inscribed in it the three requisites for public service broadcasting on Reithean lines – to inform, to educate, and to entertain.

When he assumed his new office Reith had recently been knighted. It is difficult not to see in the granting of this honour recognition by the Government of the part he had played in the General Strike of the previous year, 1926. Although the Government had taken over a newspaper press to print *The British Gazette*, Prime Minister Baldwin craftily refused to commandeer the BBC, preferring (as Reith records in his diary) 'to trust the BBC, in particular Mr Reith the managing director, to do what was best'. Reith did not disappoint, and took his editorial decisions in line with what he perceived to be the wishes of the Government. In this spirit he refused to let the Archbishop of Canterbury broadcast an ecumenical message addressed to both sides in the dispute on the casuistical grounds that 'it would be unfortunate for us to do right if it led to what we consider to be a wrong to be imposed on us' – by which he meant government control. This attitude may have pleased the Government, but it raised suspicions in sections of the public – particularly in the Labour movement and the trade unions – about the impartiality of the broadcasters.

The role of the BBC during the General Strike has passed into the mythology of broadcasting. The way that role was discharged has frequently been cited by the BBC as a demonstration of broadcasting's independence. Another reading of history sees in the events of 1926 an exemplary case of complicity with the central power of the state. It is a view borne out by an entry in Reith's diary: 'They want to be able to say that they did not commandeer us, but they know they can trust us not to be really impartial.' This complicity has remained one important – and perhaps inevitable – aspect of public service broadcasting; for it is difficult to imagine an institution functioning under a government licence to broadcast which could be an adversary or even a radical critic of the government.

The principles of public service broadcasting

As they were evolved during the inter-war years under the Reithean regime, the basic principles of public service broadcasting were as follows:

Access to the airwaves means access to a scarce public resource. Not many people or organisations can have access at any one time. Traffic in and through 'the ether' – as it was called in the early days – has to be controlled to prevent interference of one station with another and with public services like shipping, aircraft, the police, the military and government signal stations.

This privileged access carries with it certain social duties. These include the provision of a range of programmes summarised in the celebrated trinity of information, entertainment and education.

The broadcasting organisation has a duty to provide a universal signal – one that every citizen with the proper equipment should be able to pick up.

Once members of the public have acquired the licence that allows them to operate there should be no further charge for access to the programmes broadcast.

Broadcasting should not be controlled by government but by a body charged with defending the public interest – which meant the Board of Governors of the BBC.

The body which regulates broadcasting in the public interest should be non-profit-making and self-financing, paying, for instance, for capital investment out of revenue.

The role of public service broadcasting is a normative one. It cannot be morally and socially neutral. What it expresses is the consensual view of society – that body of opinion which is generally accepted by all 'sensible' people and which requires no further definition.

This summary of the Reithean principles of public service broadcasting requires some comments.

The first concerns the way in which the triple duty to inform, educate and entertain was discharged. It was only as a result of strenuous efforts by Reith that the BBC was given the right – strongly resisted by the press – to carry its own news or to broadcast commentaries on outside events. (There was one wonderfully comical occasion when the BBC broadcast the sound of the horses' hooves in a classic race but were unable to announce the winner.) As far as comment on national or international affairs was concerned, the BBC was extremely cautious and eschewed controversy. Care was taken not to offend the great dictators of the Thirties; the rise of Fascism and the economic plight of the depressed areas were not discussed. A distinguished producer who interviewed hunger-marchers was exiled to a BBC region. The incident demonstrates the strain between the professional aspirations of BBC staff (which Reith, to be fair, did sometimes support) and the desire of the authorities to limit the broadcasters' freedom to comment on current affairs, of which Reith was only too vividly aware. The result was that in a crucial period the BBC did not discharge what many would now see as its public duty: to provide a forum in which the great political and social issues of the day were debated. Churchill's wartime Minister of Information told the Commons in 1946 that Churchill had 'implored the governors of the BBC to give him an opportunity to state to the country the desperate dangers it was entering upon by the squalid policy of appeasement; but the BBC refused to give him an opportunity to speak': an accusation which a former governor had to admit was 'unfortunately true' just as it was true that Lloyd George, Churchill and Austen Chamberlain had accused the BBC of being subservient to the government whips. In fairness it has to be said that the press, with a few honourable exceptions, was equally accommodating to government pressures and that the newsreels seen by the large cinema audiences were purged of anything that might offend Hitler and rendered anodyne on social issues by self-censorship.

In the field of entertainment the Reithean tradition imposed canons of taste which were frequently at odds with the cheerful vulgarity of the British public as expressed in the music halls and variety theatres. Producers in light entertainment (what, someone asked, was heavy entertainment?) had a long list of subjects tabooed for comedians. Reith's Presbyterianism forbade entertainment on Sundays. This veto built a large audience for entertainment provided by commercial stations on the Continent like Radio Luxembourg and Radio Normandy – competition which the BBC deplored but could do little about. It required a world war and the imperative need to entertain the troops during the first boring months of that war to make the BBC change its policy.

The second criticism concerns the licence fee, which has always been a regressive tax falling equally on rich and poor. (It has to be said, however, that in a sense radio – and later television – were generally felt to be 'free'.) The proceeds of the licence fee, or such part as the Government was prepared to relinquish (for many years it kept a large part of it), were passed to the BBC. The BBC was therefore able to maintain the fiction that it was directly funded by its listeners (and later, viewers). In fact, the Government, by channelling the money from the tax, had an effective method of control.

A third concerns the function of public service broadcasting as normative – a moulder of social and political attitudes. The earlier Reitheans were clear and unashamed on this point. Broadcasting was an instrument to encourage the concept of nationhood and of the Empire. Thus a version of standard Southern English was obligatory for BBC announcers. The aim, it was stated, was to prevent the disintegration of English into 'a series of mutually unintelligible dialects and to combat the forces of disintegration which menaced not only the unity of the language but the unity of the English-speaking peoples'. In the same way the fact that 'the clock which beats time over Parliament is heard echoing in the loneliest cottage in the land' brought rural areas into direct contact with imperial institutions.

As for the material broadcast, it reflected the consensus on social questions, on politics, on taste – all matters which were assumed to be obvious to most people and certainly to the employees of the BBC. The BBC was dedicated to the promulgation of 'mainstream' views. Any views that lay outside the mainstream found difficulty in finding a voice over the air. Churchill's inability to get to the microphone is merely one outstanding example on the Right of the political spectrum.

On the positive side it has to be said that in discharging its duty to educate in the widest sense the BBC was highly successful. It had its excesses – one of them was the reading as a serial (and in the original Latin) of a whole book of Virgil's *Aeneid*; but its contribution to radio dramas, to the radio feature as a specific art-form, to the discussion of modern art and above all its systematic encouragement of music were remarkable achievements. It required courage to persevere with modern music when the broadcasting of works by a major composer like Bartok brought hysterical letters to the *Radio Times*. Admittedly the view of culture embraced was a limited one; but it earned the gratitude of many listeners. By the outbreak of the

Second World War the BBC was established as an important cultural institution with great powers of patronage, the supporter of orchestras and organiser of the Proms.

A final comment concerns the Board of Governors. They were defined by Reith as 'representatives of the public with no other interests at stake'. This was true in the sense that they had no financial holdings in the enterprise. It was also true that they were not normally appointed on a party ticket. (Political appointments have, however, become a noticeable feature with the Thatcher Government.) But that they represented interests in society was inevitable. Taken from the legendary list of the 'great and good', on which all governments draw when making such appointments, they were (and remain to this day) members of various branches of the Establishment, who while they have no defined constituencies nevertheless have at various times been representatives of powerful interests in our society such as the City, the educational establishment, industry, multi-nationals, the Foreign Office and, occasionally, one of the safer unions. They at one time included Sir Leary Constantine, who although himself black, saw nothing wrong in the black-faced coon performances of the Black and White Minstrels. Reith in fact thought of the governors as a necessary evil and was impatient of any who attempted to exercise power, to be critical and interventionist. He therefore inaugurated the pattern whereby power lay firmly in the hands of the chief executive. It is a situation which has over the years produced noticeable strains.

The shadow side

An account of public service broadcasting as embodied in the BBC would be incomplete without a reference to two matters which are not usually stressed. Both are important.

The first concerns the Licence under which the BBC operates – for like anyone else the BBC requires a licence to broadcast. That Licence is renewed from time to time; the next occasion will be in 1996 when the Charter comes up for renewal. The Licence covers many practical matters concerning the use of transmitters, the obligation not to transmit subliminal messages and the duty to broadcast an impartial daily account of the proceedings of Parliament. More importantly it specifies that the minister responsible for broadcasting may at any time require the BBC to transmit 'at the Corporation's own expense' any announcement the minister may ask it to put out. This requirement would presumably apply to announcements in a state of emergency and is perfectly natural. What is surprising is the stipulation contained in a clause which says that the minister may 'from time to time by notice in writing require the Corporation to refrain . . . from sending any matter or matter of any class specified'. In short, the minister can ban any transmission or part of a transmission. This power, when it is discussed at all, is usually described as a reserved one the use of which has been threatened more often than it has been applied. It was applied in 1988, when the Home Secretary ruled that the Corporation might not allow its viewers or listeners to hear the actual voices and words of a category of British citizens that includes members of a legal party, Sinn Fein, who have been legally elected to Parliament or to municipal councils. The grounds advanced to justify this act of censorship, which has its parallels in South Africa, are that the voices of these persons give offence to the British public.

The second point concerns security. It is difficult to discover when the practice started, but for very many years the BBC was in the habit of asking for security clearance for new members of staff and – at one time, certainly – even for contributors and performers. There is a tenable case to be made that some members of the BBC's staff must in the course of their professional duties as journalists, camera operators, engineers, have access to knowledge of a secret nature and should be checked for security. Some sort of vetting carried out with the knowledge of the staff involved and of their union representatives would have been difficult to resist. The BBC, however, had the vetting carried out secretly and when pressed pretended it was not happening. Persons who had expectations of employment found they were refused appointments. Highly competent freelance producers were unable to find work. It was a worrying example of the BBC's complicity with the state.

A socialist model?

What is surprising from today's perspective is that the British Broadcasting Corporation, operating within a public service ethos, was set up under a Conservative government and that this important step was not seen by either side of the House as a contentious matter. The explanation lies in the consensus of the time that some activities were best discharged not by business interests but by a body – a board or corporation – acting in the public interest. This is to be explained by the fact that during the First World War it had become apparent that private enterprise had not always husbanded natural resources wisely. Thus shortages of timber in wartime had led to the setting-up of the Forestry Commission to oversee the nation's woodlands in the public interest. In 1926 another public utility was regulated by the Central Electricity Board which superseded a number of private firms. Broadcasting was merely a further example of public management of a public resource supported by all political parties.

On the Labour side there was considerable approval of the organisational model evolved by the BBC. Thus Herbert Morrison, writing about the form of municipal socialism he championed – he was leader of the London County Council and set up the London Transport Board – said the BBC was an example of the type of socialist legislation which was respectable if introduced by a Conservative government but Bolshevism if introduced by a Labour one. In the same vein Hugh Dalton, who was to be Chancellor of the Exchequer in the Labour Government of 1945, wrote that the BBC was 'on its financial side a socialist model' – one which nationalised industries should copy, since it was self-financing, paid for its own developments, and did not have a budget burdened by shareholders, and because its governors, while not experts in the narrow sense, had the ability and willingness to perform the duties required of them. This complacent view tells us as much about the deficiencies in the organisational and management structures adopted in the industries nationalised by the Labour Government, of which he was to be such an important member, as it does about the BBC.

There was, however, on the Labour side a feeling that the BBC was too conservative, as was demonstrated by Reith's long fight to keep unions out of broadcasting. There was criticism too, not only from Labour, of Reith's puritanism and of his authoritarian regime – there was the famous edict that any member of staff involved in a divorce had to resign. (In his last days as Director General, mellowing perhaps, Reith had relaxed sufficiently to allow an announcer so involved to stay on, provided he did not read the religious Epilogue at the close of transmission.)

The BBC in wartime

The BBC entered the war without Reith, who had left in 1938 in search of new fields for his energies without ever finding one that matched his vast ambitions. (He aspired to be Viceroy of India.) In wartime the BBC was financed by government and – like all other communications agencies – subject to government controls. It was a period when radio enjoyed its largest and most united audiences who each night listened with anxiety or expectation to the Nine O'Clock News. It performed immense services in entertaining and informing not only the troops but also the civilian population. Variety programmes like *ITMA* (*It's That Man Again*) had an immense resonance in the audience who built catch-phrases from it into the currency of everyday language. In the field of news the BBC strove to tell as much of the truth as was possible, given the limitations of an inevitable censorship. The reporting of the BBC's war correspondents to programmes like *Radio Newsreel* were not only vivid on-the-spot journalism, often recorded in circumstances of great danger, but a great advance in the techniques of radio reporting. Before the war, at the request of government, the BBC had begun overseas broadcasts in English and a number of foreign languages; but in these transmissions, too, it wisely aimed by and large to tell as much of the truth as possible. It was the accuracy of the BBC news, which chronicled losses as well as victories, and its refusal to indulge in deception, that gave it such authority in Occupied Europe. The Voice of London was listened to with attention; often in situations of great danger, not only to follow military developments but to hear coded messages like 'The cigarettes have arrived' – which meant that an arms-drop to a resistance group near Siena (to which Stuart Hood belonged) was imminent.

It has to be said, on the other hand, that J. B. Priestley's immensely popular wartime postcripts to the news were judged to be too left-wing and were discontinued and that Beveridge, the liberal economist whose report to the Government laid the basis of the Welfare State, was not able to comment on his plan to the national audience. Churchill considered the discussion of post-war society as a distraction from the war effort. The complicity with Government remained.

The post-war years and the rise of television

Television had begun in 1936, one of its early successes being, significantly – given the lavish attention to royal occasions which were to become the hallmark of BBC Television – the Coronation of George VI. The service was cut off just before war was declared in September 1939 because German bombers might use the London transmitter at Alexandra Palace as a beacon; the service did not resume until 1946.

In the post-war years there was a feeling of anticlimax in radio and an unwillingness to reassess the role of the medium. The only major change – it was an important one – was the inauguration of the Third Programme, which was quickly copied by other European broadcasters. There was a reluctance to accept that television was a more effective medium in most fields of entertainment and to work out what radio could do most effectively at a time when the audience was moving over to television and changing its listening habits. Gradually and against very considerable resistance from executives brought up on the pure milk of the pre-war Reithean tradition, television won the upper hand. The struggle to have a television news service that was not dominated by the thinking of executives used only to radio and therefore fearful and suspicious of the moving image was a long one and symptomatic of the difficulties the new medium encountered.

BBC Television, although its audience continued to grow as sets became cheaper, also found it difficult to shake off the traditions of the past. It was London-centred. It catered for the tastes of a metropolitan, middle-class audience. Its tone was genteel. It certainly was not attuned to the large new working-class audience who showed their ingratitude by switching to commercial television when it was introduced in 1955. Within a few years the commercial rival ITV would bring had brought the BBC's audience share down to around 30 per cent and lower.

The monopoly questioned

Although the services provided during the war had strengthened the reputation of the BBC as a national institution, in the post-war years its monopoly came increasingly under fire. Some critics saw in the situation 'the danger of excessive power over men's [sic] thoughts concentrated in a single organisation working out in complacency, lack of imagination, and deadly uniformity of public opinion'. To this the remedy was seen as competition between three or more Corporations, each with national coverage. Others saw a danger of 'excessive size in the present Corporation and of unwieldiness'. The answer proposed was a functional break-up of the monopoly into home sound broadcasting (the word 'radio' was not yet in generally accepted use), television and overseas broadcasting, each in independent hands. A third line of criticism came from representatives of Scotland and Wales, who objected to central control from London and the imposition of English cultural values. The answer, said these critics, was separate corporations to ensure that national characteristics were not obliterated. Yet another objection to the monopoly came from those who made their living by broadcasting, whether as employees or performers. They feared the power of the monopoly over their lives. They wanted more than one employer, more than one market.

These proposals are all contained in the report drawn up in 1951 by a committee chaired by Lord Beveridge, the author of the Beveridge plan and father of the Welfare State. Its remit was to look at the future of broadcasting. What is interesting about the proposals is that they emerged so soon after the war and that they pointed to debates that would in one way or another continue down to the present day. Nor were they the only issues raised that refused to die. Others were access (though the word was not used) through a 'Hyde Park Corner of the Air' for which the BBC's editorial rules would be relaxed, greater public involvement in decision-making, sponsorship, financing through direct taxation, and devolution.

While sympathising with the critics, the committee turned down their suggestions, not because it did not very largely agree with them, but because it felt that their ends could be better served by a single chartered corporation that would be required to make steady progress towards greater decentralisation, devolution, and diversity.

Beveridge's committee found it less easy to reach an agreed conclusion on advertising. A majority was against it on the grounds that it would 'sooner or later endanger the traditions of public service, high standards and impartiality, which have been built up in the past 25 years'. One member, however, saw a means of avoiding the dangers of monopoly, 'of giving traders a new facility and indeed of improving the broadcasting service'. It was sponsorship – the system whereby advertisers funded programmes. There should, he felt, be a continuing public service financed by the licence with alongside it a national and local commercial service. Others sat on the fence and were for advertising if it were confined to a 'controlled and limited advertisement hour' separated off like the advertising columns of a newspaper. Once more the lines of the debate were being clearly drawn.

Looked at from today's perspective, the most important voice in the debate was that of the Conservative politician, Selwyn Lloyd, later to be a Conservative Chancellor, and Foreign Minister at the time of Suez, but whose contribution to the history of broadcasting is probably his only enduring monument. What he did as a member of the Beveridge Committee, in which his was the solitary voice in support of sponsorship, was to append to its findings a minority report. In it he supported the idea of a commercial broadcasting operation on the grounds that 'independent competition will be healthy for broadcasting'.

The Report appeared when the Labour Government which had come to power in 1945 was at its last gasp; but the Government was in agreement with its basic conclusions. It is not surprising, however, that the Conservative Government that followed was not and proceeded to announce that it had 'come to the conclusion that in the expanding field of television provision should be made to permit some element of competition when the calls on capital resources at present needed for purposes of greater national importance make this feasible'. But although the BBC was for the first time about to face competition, it was not in the event to be confronted by unfettered commercialism. When it arrived, the new commercial network – which, to the fury of the BBC, was euphemistically baptised Independent Television (ITV) – was also bound by the norms of public service broadcasting.

TWO

The Breaking of the BBC's Monopoly

The Television Act 1954, which brought ITV into existence, was the result of an extraordinary and unremitting lobbying campaign such as had not been seen before in Britain but which presaged a new approach to methods of influencing public opinion. Spearheaded by a group of Conservative MPs, it has been described as 'perhaps the most remarkable exhibition of political lobbying this country has ever seen – for there has been no disguise of the commercial interests involved'. Its activities included those of a body called the Popular Television Association, which organised letters to the editors (often of local papers), the texts of which were identical or slightly varied, but which in the case of one batch of nineteen all came from the same address in London. It was an important feather in the cap of the advertisers' lobby that it won the support of a distinguished ex-BBC executive, Norman Collins, who as head of BBC Television had seen his efforts to promote the service thwarted by bureaucracy and prejudice.

The passing of the Act through Parliament was preceded by an intense public debate in which prominent figures were ranged for and against the BBC. The terms in which it was conducted often verged on hysteria on both sides. Thus in the Lords, Reith, now ennobled, compared the coming of television to the arrival of the bubonic plague in these islands, and a well-known comedian, much used by the BBC, accused it improbably of screening 'foul films' and 'boosting bawdy books'. What emerged was that the BBC had many critics – not to say enemies – and that it had contributed to its unpopularity by a lack of response to a changing public, by its mandarin attitudes and by the maintenance of some of the negative sides of the Reithean tradition.

The two main political parties were divided. Among the Conservatives those who would now be called 'wets' defended the concept of public service, which reflected their own often patrician views on public duty; others enthusiastically welcomed the breaking of the monopoly and the opportunities of commercialism. The Labour Party, in its turn, was partly supportive of the BBC as a non-profit-making public service institution; partly critical because of its closeness to the Establishment and because it was felt to be remote from life – at least as most Labour supporters experienced it – and unresponsive to their tastes and interests.

There was, however, general agreement on both sides of the House – an agreement that was reflected in the terms of the Act – that the excesses of commercial television in the United States should be avoided. Politicians had seen American television for themselves; it had alarmed them. In particular there was a determination to forbid sponsorship of programmes, since sponsorship, as practised in the States, gave the manufacturers great power over programme and editorial decisions. Nor were the screens in Britain to carry as many commercials or carry them so frequently. There was to be a regulatory body overseeing commercial television in the public interest – something more effective than the Federal Communications Commission in the States which (to use today's buzz-word) had a very light touch when regulating the intensely competitive American networks.

This body was the Independent Television Authority (ITA), whose members were drawn from the same list of 'the great and good' as the BBC Board and were equally unrepresentative of 'the public'. The Authority was in law 'the broadcaster'. A public service body, it was enjoined in the terms of the Act to discharge three duties: to inform, educate and entertain. What had, in effect, been created was a duopoly within which the BBC and the ITA operated to the same basic rules.

The Television Act 1954

The Act was very specific in its requirements. Thus it was laid down that the programmes broadcast by the Authority – the ITA – or its agents should maintain 'a proper balance in their subject matter and a high general standard of quality'; nothing must 'offend against good taste and decency' (which the Authority was to have the difficult task of defining); neither was anything to be broadcast likely to encourage or incite to crime or to lead to disorder or to be offensive to public feeling. News was to be presented with 'due accuracy and impartiality'. Impartiality was also to be observed in matters of political or industrial controversy or in comments on current public policy; which was not to be taken to mean that 'properly balanced discussion or debates where the persons taking part express opinions and put forward arguments of a political character' were to be excluded.

Fears about the effects of advertising on the screen were met by the ruling that there was to be no sponsorship by advertisers. And the amount of space allocated to advertising was not to be 'so great as to detract from the value of programmes as a medium of entertainment, instruction and information'. In American television, advertisements appeared in frequent clusters, often interrupting the flow of a programme; here advertisements were only to be inserted at the beginning or end of a programme or in 'natural breaks'. The Authority was instructed to reach an agreement with the Postmaster-General, the minister who was then responsible for broadcasting, to decide how frequently the commercial breaks could come. In the event, the interval between the breaks was set at approximately twenty minutes.

What is interesting about the ground-rules laid down by the Act is that there are no such detailed prescriptions in the Charter of the BBC. It is clear that there was considerable distrust of commercial broadcasting and a perceived need to curb any possible excesses in advance. In such matters the BBC was seen

to have demonstrated its dependability. There was an un-
mistakable feeling that a distinction was being made between
the gentlemen and the players.

The network

It was left to the ITA to decide how commercial television
should be organised. It decided that there should be what was in
the early days called a federal system. It came to be known as the
Independent Television Network (ITV), composed of programme companies who had contracted to supply programmes
to the Authority, which was, in law, 'the broadcaster'.

The contractors

The United Kingdom was divided up into a series of franchise
areas and interested parties were invited to apply for contracts to
broadcast to a particular area. The object was twofold: to
encourage competition between the franchise-holders and to
promote regional identity. Neither aim was notably successful.
Applicants had to demonstrate that they were financially sound;
and that they had an acceptable programme policy, and
executives capable of putting that policy into practice. What was
important was that the Authority's choice was therefore not
necessarily based on financial considerations alone but on its
estimation of how well successful candidates would discharge
their duties under the Act.

   Various safeguards to prevent contracts from going to foreign
interests or to persons with competing interests were built into
the Act. Thus persons not ordinarily resident in the United
Kingdom, the Isle of Man or the Channel Islands could not
apply for a franchise nor could some other categories like
advertising agents, who would have too great a commercial
stake in the operation and might be tempted to maximise
audiences without regard for the principles of public service.

Their selection

When granting the franchises the Authority could and did lay down conditions affecting the composition of a group awarded a contract. Thus it might say that local interests must be more effectively represented on the company board or offered a share in the venture. It might oblige the successful applicants to reach an agreement with one of the unsuccessful applicants so as to strengthen some aspect of the operation. Once the contract had been granted the Act laid down that it could not in whole or in part be assigned to anyone else without the Authority's permission. This aimed to prevent take-overs and changes of ownership. The Authority also had the power to terminate a contract if its terms were not for any reason fulfilled; the franchises were not granted in perpetuity and came to be reviewed at specified intervals. They were not necessarily renewed. Today only Granada survives from the original applicants in 1954. Some have gone out of business or amalgamated with other contractors; some have not had their contracts renewed. Today there are fifteen regional contractors and TV AM, which is not regional.

Competition?

The authority had the duty laid on it by the 1954 Act to encourage 'adequate competition' between the programme contractors to supply programmes; but that competition, as we shall see, was not obvious in practice; nor is it clear, given their regional organisation, how they could compete any more than water authorities can be expected to compete in any meaningful way today.

The duties of a contractor

Each successful contractor had the monopoly of advertising in its own franchise area and in exchange was required to cater for the special interests of its local audience. The contractor paid the Authority a large rental for the privilege of its local monopoly. The contractors' revenue – and profits – stemmed from spot advertising of either a local or a national nature. Since contractors had a monopoly in their franchise areas they were able to dictate the rates per minute for advertising airtime.

The role of the Authority

These payments furnished the Authority with revenue which allowed it to build and maintain the infrastructure that made broadcasting possible. In that infrastructure the transmitters were a crucial item. The Authority therefore required a staff of engineers to whom were added officers responsible for audience research and, above all, a considerable staff for supervising what went on the air whether in the shape of programmes or advertisements. The Act was quite specific on this point and laid down that the Authority could demand to see scripts and to be informed about not only the contents but 'the visual images and sounds'. It had, as a logical corollary, the power to forbid the broadcasting of any programme or part of a programme or advertisement.

For its part the Authority was subject to powers in the hands of the responsible minister who might – as in the case of the BBC – order it to broadcast material or forbid it to do so. The Authority has, therefore, like the BBC, in recent times obeyed the ruling that viewers may not hear the voices of legally elected representatives of Sinn Fein, the political arm of the IRA.

The news service

The news service for the network was to be provided by Independent Television News (ITN), a company owned jointly by the contractors. It was to become one of the outstanding successes of the new system.

No institution remains unchanged over more than thirty years, but the Authority – which changed its name to the Independent *Broadcasting* Authority (IBA) with the introduction of Independent (i.e. commercial) Local Radio in 1973 – still has the same powers (indeed they have been strengthened meantime) and still oversees what is essentially the same system. These were, and are, wide powers if the Authority chooses to use them.

A licence to print money

If one talks to the executives who were involved in the early days of commercial television one hears stories of difficulties, of financial crises, of one contractor bailing out another which found itself suddenly unable to pay its staff. Such stories have entered into the legendary history of ITV. Undoubtedly there were difficult moments and heavy losses in the first days; but the new network's popular approach, typified at its best by the way ITN used less pompous language and was less inhibited than the BBC, paid off. ITV, as we have seen, began to pull much of the audience away from the BBC. The result was a large advertising revenue – so large that the proprietor of STV, Scotland's largest commercial station, felt able to say in a moment of frankness that a television franchise was a licence to print money. Twelve years after the system came into being, one company (which has since ceased to be a contractor) had made total profits of £52 million from a starting capital of £500,000; there were other comparable figures. It was the clear evidence that great wealth was being generated by some of the contractors (and often being siphoned off into other enterprises rather than being put back into television) that led a Conservative government in 1963 to impose on the contractors a special tax on advertising revenue: the levy. The levy is still in force; but since 1974 it has been charged on profits, each company paying 66 per cent of its profits in levy after deduction of a fee slice. The levy is additional to normal company tax. The levy is greatly resented by contractors. It has, however, not prevented them from continuing to make large profits.

The ITV network in operation

The Act wished to encourage competition in providing programmes for the network. But in fact the system came to be
dominated by the 'network companies', so called because they
have a specific obligation to provide programmes for broadcasting throughout the network. (They have been compared to
medieval barons and sometimes behave like them.) They are
five in number and today are Granada, Central, London
Weekend Television (LWT), Thames and Yorkshire – that is to
say, those contractors which are rich enough to have invested
capital in the considerable resources, like electronic studios and
film equipment, required to produce programmes covering
drama, soap operas, entertainment, current affairs and outside
broadcasts. There is a second string of contractors which
includes companies like STV (Scottish Television), Anglia, and
TVS (Television South), which have contrived to obtain access
to the network for their programmes (Anglia, for instance, by
specialising in nature programmes). Then come the small
regional companies like Border, Grampian or Channel which
serve small areas and have correspondingly low revenues. The
difficulty those smaller companies have met in competing for an
occasional showing on the network has been a source of friction
within the system. On the other hand, the strength of ITV from
an early stage in its existence was that it encouraged local news
and local magazine programmes, which have considerable
importance in that they give a platform to local politicians and
local interests. This was an area the BBC was slow to move into
because of its metropolitan bias.

Curiously, for an organisation set up to encourage competition, the ITV network is not based on competition between the
programme companies that have acquired the contracts for the
various area franchises. The network schedule is, in fact, a
mosaic of programmes 'offered', in the main, by the big network
companies. While it is theoretically possible for other companies to refuse, they are unlikely to do so, and most companies

carry most of the network programmes most of the time. Payment has then to be made by any station that carries a programme to the company which has produced and financed it – such as *Coronation Street*, which is a Granada production but is carried by the entire network. The methods involved attracted the interest of the Prices and Incomes Board which gave this account of it in 1970:

> This (non-profit-making) principle is reflected in the fact that the programmes made by any network company have to be offered around the system, not at prices reflecting the maximum figure achievable but rather at fixed tariffs reflecting the NARAL (net advertising revenue after levy) of the contractor in which the programme is to be screened. Under this arrangement one company may have to pay more than £1,400 for an hour's programming, while another is able to take it for a little over £50.

The real competition was not within the network but against the BBC. Here it was in general beneficial. The BBC was shaken out of its complacency by services which were sometimes more adventurous, less stuffy and certainly more popular than the Corporation's. The ITN news service was an outstanding example which caused the BBC's share of the audience to slip disastrously. Its decision to try to restore parity without sacrificing programme standards – in which it was successful – was necessary not only to restore staff morale but to prevent politicians from arguing that citizens should not be taxed to pay for a service which only a third of the population watched. (There were members of the public who objected to having to pay the licence fee on the grounds that they only ever watched ITV; but the courts ruled that viewing habits were irrelevant because the licence fee was a legal requirement if one wished to own and operate a receiver.)

There was one important characteristic which the competing organisations until recently had in common: they were vertically integrated. That is to say, both the BBC and those ITV companies with productive capacity produced the bulk of their output in their own studios, using their own production staff, producers, directors, camera crews and so on. This meant that there was very little scope for independent producers, who could have a difficult time if they were not prepared to join the BBC or an ITV company and – by becoming staff members – lose certain freedoms. It is true that the existence of the ITV companies did allow for a certain liberating movement of skilled and creative people from one competitor to the other; but the BBC was believed (with justice) to have on its payroll producers who produced very little but had all the advantages that come from being institutionalised. With time there would be growing pressure for this state of affairs to be reformed.

The Television Act 1964: the Authority is given teeth

There was considerable feeling in the early years of ITV that the Authority had an unduly cosy relationship with the contractors and did not do enough to control or curb their programme policies. This feeling was reflected in the Television Act 1964 which became law nine years after commercial television began. It is longer and more detailed than the 1954 Act. This reflects concern among some of the public at what was seen as lack of judgement in screening violent American series. (American television is notoriously more tolerant of violence, while being prudish about sex.) This led to the Authority being instructed to draw up a code setting out the rules to be observed when showing violence on the screen, particularly when young people might be watching, and to ensure that the code was observed in all programmes. Today this code is a detailed and bulky document which covers offences to good taste and decency, the portrayal of violence, accuracy, privacy, fairness and impartiality, crime and social behaviour, interviews with criminals, interviews with children, 'trial by television', and a host of other matters.

Similarly the Authority was instructed to draw up a code of

advertising practice; this it proceeded to do as (in its own words) 'one of the country's official instruments of consumer protection'. With that in mind it drew up a code which has been expanded and modified over the years. As it stands today it contains a wide range of provisions, instructions and taboos.

First and foremost is a provision against sponsorship to the effect that no programme may state or even hint that it has been supplied or suggested by an advertiser. Commercials are to be clearly distinguishable and separate from programmes; so, for example, presenters may not – as they sometimes do in the United States – advertise goods (thus lending their authority and that of their organisation to the product). There may be no subliminal advertising. Nor may there be political advertising, advertising relating to an industrial dispute, religious advertising or advertising that takes sides in a matter of public controversy. (But where does this leave the Government's advertising campaigns in support of privatisation?)

Beyond that there are rules governing protection of privacy, the offer of prizes, stridency – commercials must not be excessively loud. Superstition must not be exploited. Various categories of goods and services are excluded, ranging from matrimonial agencies, betting shops and fortune-tellers to undertakers. (The British viewing public has shown itself sensitive about contraception and death.) Children must not misbehave in commercials or take risks. Financial advertising is strictly controlled. Cigarette advertising is banned. There is a long section dealing with alcoholic drinks including the rule that drinking must not be associated with masculinity. The advertising of medicines is equally painstakingly limited. All in all, it is a comprehensive and enlightened code. Some day, perhaps, it will be as stringent about sexism as it is about misbehaviour in children.

In line with its firmer touch, the Act made one extremely important rule: that the programme schedules of the contractors were to be drawn up in consultation with the Authority and were not to be embarked on without the Authority's approval. This provision in effect confirmed the Authority's power to mandate certain programmes – that is to say, to insist that they be scheduled at times laid down by the Authority – and to insist as well that both the network schedule and the local schedules carried a proper mix of material. This effectively prevented the contractors from attempting to maximise audiences by scheduling entertainment programmes with high ratings across the peak evening viewing hours. Programmes dealing with current affairs, documentaries and similar broadly informative programmes had to be scheduled at times which meant that a large audience had the chance to watch them if they so wished. The Reithean principles of public service broadcasting were still alive.

The Act also revealed concern at the possibility of newspaper interests acquiring shareholdings in programme companies, which might lead to a monopoly of media ownership. The Act laid down that the minister might intervene if he thought that holdings of this kind had led or were likely to lead to results contrary to the public interest. The problem of relations between the press and broadcasting went back to the very earliest days when, for example, the newspaper proprietors attempted to prevent the BBC from putting out a news service of any kind. When the BBC persisted in doing so it thought it wise to set the main bulletin at 6 o'clock (where it has remained) because by then the last edition of the evening newspapers would be on the streets.

The relationship between the press and the broadcasting media has continued, as we shall see, to be an issue up to the present day. It surfaced again in legislation passed in 1973 which gave the Authority, now renamed the Independent Broadcasting Authority, powers to franchise and oversee local radio stations. The spread of local commercial radio would mean competition for advertising with local papers. To ensure that they were not put out of business by the new competitors, local newspapers were expressly permitted to acquire shareholdings in the new stations so long as they did not obtain control over the company.

On the other hand, there was concern – it cropped up in the report of a Royal Commission on the Press published in 1977 – about the possibility of media power being concentrated in too few hands in a period when take-overs were becoming common and newspapers and publishing houses being traded. The same Act therefore laid down that a contractor providing television for a specific franchise area may not also provide a local radio service.

A regulated commercial system

One motive behind the introduction of ITV in 1955 had been to allow scope for commercial interests and the forces of the market. In the event these forces and interests were highly regulated. It says a great deal for the profitability of the system that it flourished financially in spite of being hemmed in by rules and regulations. It is worth recalling what these regulations were.

1. There was a limit on the amount of commercial advertising, set at six minutes in the hour, commercials being permitted only at natural breaks at roughly twenty-minute intervals; today this limit stands at an average of seven minutes per hour;
2. audiences could not be maximised at all times even though a large audience lowers the 'cost per thousand [viewers]', which is traditionally a crucial term in calculating the effectiveness of the programme from the advertisers' point of view;
3. contracting companies could not be acquired or taken over or otherwise varied in composition without the permission of the Authority;
4. a steep levy was imposed on the contractors' revenue from advertising – a tax which was changed in 1974 to a levy on profits;
5. contracts are granted for a limited period and are subject to revision and renewal.

These regulations mean that, to quote a report on the financing of broadcasting by the Home Affairs Committee of Parliament, 'the companies' ability to maximise profits is to some extent limited by the obligations of public service broadcasting . . . and their contracts with the IBA'. For example, the report goes on, 'the programmes must maintain a high standard, there must be adequate provision of news and a certain proportion of programmes must be of British origin'.

These restrictions and regulations have not prevented the contractors from prospering.

As to the quality of the service provided, this highly regulated commercial system was to produce not only programmes which included (especially in the early days) a good deal of dross (as have those of the BBC, which found itself competing for a popular audience) but also outstanding contributions to many television genres. The duopoly operating according to the ground rules of public service broadcasting seemed to be working reasonably well.

THREE

New Approaches to Broadcasting

In the Sixties, British broadcasting under the duopoly was well-established and confident. It was a period when the two broadcasting organisations each had a share of about half the audience although the figure fluctuated from time to time to the accompaniment of claims and counter-claims and contradictory figures from the rival audience research units. On the technical side, colour was introduced along with a picture that had better definition. The number of television homes was rising steadily and would by the end of the decade have more or less reached saturation point. It was also the time when television became accepted as a serious and important news medium, as the present Chairman of ITN recalls.

There was some very eventful news in those days – no satellites of course – but a lot of news. I mean the Kennedy election, the U2 [the American spy-plane] affair, the summits, Khrushchev and Kennedy; but I think that television news really came of age with the Cuban missile crisis which was in 1962. First of all, it was a very pictorial issue in the sense that Kennedy in mobilising American forces and raising the issue in a dramatic radio and television speech said 'Look, here are pictures of missile sites in Cuba' and 'Here are pictures taken by reconnaissance aircraft of rockets on the decks of Soviet freighters on their way to Havana'. That was an amazing week of huge international tension when the world faced the possibility of a nuclear exchange. It was a real crisis and it was moving so fast in the way that modern communications can with the exchange of notes between Moscow and Washington. Newspapers were almost out of date by the time they got loaded into the vans and television news – not just ITN but the BBC as well and US television – was really up to the minute in those days showing the picture, showing what was happening, explaining what was going on. And people turned to television and said: 'What's happened since I saw the last news programme three hours ago?' It seems to me that that was a moment of sudden puberty for television news when it ceased to be a kind of rather enhanced newsreel and turned into the place you go to first for the latest news.

The growing audience to which ITN addressed itself meant that ITV could win large ratings, which made the advertisers happy. The late Fifties had seen the fastest growth in total advertising expenditure ever seen in the United Kingdom. By 1960 commercial television had captured 22 per cent of the total expenditure while the press's share fell from 87 to 70 per cent.

The Pilkington Committee

The BBC, too, was in good shape. It had emerged well – some members of staff felt embarrassingly well – from examination by yet another government committee on broadcasting, headed by the paternalistic glass manufacturer, Sir Harry Pilkington, which reported in 1962. One member of the Committee was Richard Hoggart, the academic and adult education expert and author of an important book on culture and society, *The Uses of Literacy*, which discusses the possible interplay between material improvement and cultural loss. His hand was evident in the arguments set out in its report and the terms in which it was drafted.

If the Pilkington Report was strong in its commendation of the BBC and its dedication to Reithean principles (suitably updated to match the less repressive atmosphere of the times) it was unsparing in its condemnation of the IBA and commercial television in which it detected a fundamental weakness; which was that it was intended to serve two contradictory purposes. One was to provide a television service which would realise 'as fully as possible' the purposes of broadcasting. These the Report proceeded to define. The first was that the broadcaster must 'use the medium with an acute awareness of its power to influence values and moral standards'. It ought therefore to respect the public right 'to choose from amongst the widest possible range of subject matter' and should be constantly on the watch for and ready to try the new and unusual. But the second purpose of commercial television was to provide a service to advertisers. In the view of the Committee the two purposes of independent television do not coincide. This came as no surprise to the Committee because 'the purposes – and the effects – of broadcasting are not such that it can be left to the ordinary processes of commerce'. Nor, as the Report spells out, do the normal laws of commerce apply to it.

> The product [of broadcasting] should be a service which fully realises the purposes of broadcasting. But, if the broadcasters fail materially, no direct and immediate fall in revenue results. That corrective, the normal consequence of a failure to provide adequate service in the world of commerce, does not operate. It cannot operate because the BBC is financed by licence revenue and because independent television is not financed by the sale of programmes to the public, but by the sale of advertising time to advertisers. In neither case is there a direct or immediate financial incentive to realise the purposes of broadcasting.

This view of the economics of broadcasting would be discussed from a very different point of view twenty years later when financing of the BBC came to be examined by yet another government-appointed committee.

The strongly expressed approval of its record in the

Pilkington Report was greatly encouraging to the BBC and its morale. On the economic level it was also buoyant, partly because of the increased licence revenue (the steady rise in sales of sets meant a corresponding rising graph of licence revenue), partly because in 1963 the Government at last gave the Corporation all the licence fee (£4 in those pre-inflationary years) less £1 excise duty. It was also editorially confident and competing well with ITV. BBC2 was started. It was a major development in British television. Conceived of as a channel which would be complementary to BBC1, which was caught up in competition with ITV for the popular audience, it embarked on a remarkable output of drama, arts and music programmes, while not neglecting more popular topics like wild-life. By a policy of cross-trailing at programme junctions the BBC aimed to keep viewers within the BBC's orbit; for although some of BBC2's viewers inevitably came from BBC1, the aim was to retain a global audience as large as that BBC1 had enjoyed.

Radio was reorganised, not without much anguish on the part of some BBC producers who wrote to *The Times* to protest at what they felt was the abandonment of Reithean principles. What concerned them was the targeting of different and separate audiences by Radios 1, 2, 3 and 4 – a policy that ran counter to the long-established view that audiences should be exposed to the unfamiliar, the new, and so led to widen their tastes. There were others, however, who felt that BBC Radio was emerging from the doldrums of the Fifties and moving – where popular music was concerned – into areas of broadcasting in the early Sixties that had been left to the offshore pirates like Radio Caroline, which was at last declared illegal in 1967.

What the BBC did not succeed in doing was to persuade any government to recognise it formally as 'the national instrument of broadcasting' with all the prestige and authority that that title would have conferred. Moreover, stresses and strains began to appear in the relationship between the BBC and the political parties. The Corporation had for long taken the view that it was likely to be out of favour with the party in opposition, that this was in the nature of things and had to be endured. But signs began to emerge, particularly when Harold Wilson was prime minister, that a government in power might react strongly against what was seen as the arrogance of the Corporation. Wilson's appointment of Lord Hill, formerly a Tory minister, who had been chairman of IBA, as chairman of the BBC Board of Governors was seen as an unusual political move which had a double objective: to alter the balance of power between the Chairman and the Director General and to force the resignation of Sir Hugh Greene, who in that post had encouraged his staff to be adventurous in programme-making and in their willingness to question political motives even in ministers of the highest rank on such matters as British support of American policies in Vietnam.

Public service broadcasting faces criticism

Naturally, the broadcasting institutions were not exempt from the effects of the ferment of ideas that inspired the radicalism of the Sixties. The cosy certainties of the duopoly came under attack from many quarters as the decade progressed. Within the broadcasting institutions there was growing impatience among programme-makers at the restrictions imposed by the system, a feeling that there must be other and more liberal or more radical ways of managing the broadcasting media. It was a time when models of co-ownership, of involvement of workers in management and of more democratic control, were much discussed. BBC producers, in particular, felt frustration at the growth of bureaucracy and administrative power – a result of the sudden expansion of the Corporation at this time – which resulted in what they experienced as a diminution of their role as men and women who could at certain levels help to determine policy. Where ITV was concerned there was, on the one hand, impatience with the IBA's apparent reluctance to stand up to the most powerful companies which appeared to go their own way in terms of corporate policies and, on the other, resentment at

the increasing interference of the IBA in details of programme-
making. There was among producers in both BBC and ITV a
growing feeling that their masters were losing their nerve.
Politicians of a conservative cast of mind in all parties, for their
part, began to see the spectre of 'producer power'.

An idea not only of the feelings abroad among professional
broadcasters and of the terms in which they formulated their
criticisms but of the heady atmosphere of the times can be had
from an excerpt from the first edition of *Open Secret*, a journal
produced in 1968 by the Free Communications Group. This was
a loose association of journalists, producers and workers in the
various branches of the communications media, who had 'many
aims and interests in common' and who now proceeded to make
lively interventions in the discussion of broadcasting policy.

> We have a common interest [said the journal] in the
> quality, organisation and control of the huge
> communications industry in this country . . . The media
> are now largely locked up in enormous multi-media
> concerns which administer a portfolio of holdings in
> every branch of the industry . . . Granada [the franchise
> holder in the North-West of England] is in television,
> publishing, garages, rent-a-flower and grocery stores.

As an alternative to commercial television, the BBC, they
find, offers scant solace.

> As everyone knows it is a rigid and fiercely hierarchic
> corporate state, with all the minute gradations, checks,
> protocols and rungs for which the Chinese Imperial Civil
> Service was once justly famous. But this structure
> contains real centres of power, and at this time the
> centres are in a process of retrenchment and effacement
> before the Establishment. Their genuflections and
> concessions need to be minutely recorded.
>   No one would suggest that Milton's *Areopagitica* is the
> charter of the US communications industry. But against
> the imminent arrival of commercial radio here it is worth
> noting that in New York there is a highly popular radio

station run by radicals. It is financed by contributions from its audience. There are no other restraints. Where is the equivalent freedom in this country? Here decisions always devolve to owners, politicians and upper management; upper management being, as we know, always finks, passing the buck till it is safely stowed in the company safe.

The whole debate about what free communication can be has never really taken place. It has been surrendered to Royal Commissions and pieties about nationalisation.

The Sixties and Seventies also saw increasing attention by academics to the media and the growth of interest in communication studies. The achievement of these academic researchers was that in spite of bureaucratic obstacles some of them contrived to penetrate into the heart of an institution like the BBC to conduct sociological examinations which the broadcasting professionals found hard to understand and deeply unsettling when they did understand them, for they called in question the concepts and the ideology on which their professional practices were based, practices which to them seemed to be merely commonsensical and therefore unquestionable. What the sociologists examined was the way in which the broadcasting institutions worked and found that they had produced a 'new priesthood', which felt itself to be the guardians of the media. The concepts of 'impartiality' and 'objectivity' to which the BBC and IBA adhered were questioned and the political assumptions behind them critically examined. What, for instance, were the unstated assumptions which informed the judgements of the people who made editorial policy? How did they make these judgements? How did they know what language to use to describe people and events in the news, language which by its nature could not be neutral?

One of the studies which the professionals found most difficult to take was *Bad News*, produced in 1976 by the Glasgow University Media Group, which firmly stated that 'contrary to the claims, conventions, and culture of television journalism, the news is not a neutral product. For television

news is a cultural artifact; it is a sequence of socially manufactured messages, which carry many of the culturally dominant
assumptions of our society. From the accents of the newscasters
to the vocabulary of camera angles; from who gets on and what
questions they are asked, via selection of stories to presentation
of bulletins, the news is a highly mediated product.' The most
important role of the broadcasters was that of agenda-setting –
the ability to give certain events public prominence whilst
ignoring others, which is 'crucial in considering the news
operation'. This, they argued, was not a value-free exercise; the
contention by the professionals that within the limits of time and
money their coverage is 'objective' is based on the idea that facts
exist outside a frame of reference. The reaction of the broadcasters to the work, which analysed newscasts in terms that were
common and largely unquestioned currency in academic
studies, was angry and puzzled.

Outside academic circles other questions were being asked,
such as with what right did the broadcasters – who were
generally white, male and middle-class – decide who might or
might not have access to the screen or microphone? What were
the rights of interviewees? Why did opinions always have to be
mediated by some safe interviewer or panel chairman? Why
could members of the public not express their views directly –
have access to the media? Was not the concept of 'balance', to
which both BBC and ITV subscribed, a way of fudging issues?
Was the television audience not adult enough to hear clearly
stated, unmediated, committed expressions of opinion? How
truly impartial were the professionals anyway, since they were
preponderantly of the same social class, the same educational
background, shared the same idea of a political consensus?
Broadcasters in Holland, Sweden and Denmark had much
greater freedom than those in Britain. Was there not a danger in
the ratings war that broadcasters might lose sight of important
minorities? Ought not these minorities which were definable in
terms of sexuality, ethnicity and class, be given more space on
the air?

Tony Benn, who once said broadcasting was too important to be left to the broadcasters and had himself been a BBC television producer, took up the issue at a symposium at the University of Manchester in 1972. He was of the opinion that the real question was not whether programmes were good or serious, balanced or truthful, but whether they allowed people to reflect to each other their diversity of interests, opinions, grievances, hopes and attitudes, and to talk over their differences at length.

> The publishing function [of broadcasting] has been very largely neglected until very recently and almost the whole output on all channels has been devised and presented under editorial direction. This has had serious political consequences. Since those with something constructive to say, together with others expressing discontents in society, have been denied the right to publish their views, some important grievances have festered until they have reached explosion point. And when the explosion comes the mass media have been only too ready to give extensive coverage to the demonstrations and violence . . . What they should have been doing was to provide ample time for these views to be expressed beforehand so as to provide society with the feedback essential to correct its errors before they do too much damage, and the chance to understand future choices by having the alternatives presented to them.

He was unimpressed by the argument that the public would switch off out of boredom. 'Are we to accept the ratings,' he asked 'as the final determinant of what should and should not be broadcast?' and went on to argue that while some cultural minorities are well catered for others are not. 'What is evidently not accepted is that the minority who are really interested in a penetrating study of social problems – industrial relations, race relations or Ulster – are equally entitled to have access to the information they need to help them form a judgment.'

The reference to Northern Ireland was particularly relevant, for the social and political situation had long been neglected by both the BBC and the IBA. There had been little on the television screens or on radio – no analysis of Protestant gerrymandering (the manipulation of electoral boundaries) or of discrimination over housing and jobs, for instance, no exploration of the grievances of the nationalist and Catholic minorities – to prepare people in mainland Britain for the crisis that erupted in Ulster in the Sixties with the repression of the civil rights movement. Once the crisis could no longer be concealed, strict censorship prevented the British public from forming a view on the issues based on the statements and opinions of all the parties involved in the conflict. Both the IBA and the BBC were guilty of suppressing debate and reporting; which was often justified on the dubious (and unchallengeable) grounds of security.

Other fundamental questions began to be asked about the way the controlling bodies functioned. Why, for instance, should the IBA, when it allocated broadcasting franchises, not make a public hearing part of the normal proceedings for awarding a contract? It was, after all, giving access to a public resource. The point was elaborated in the report of a commission on broadcasting published in 1972 by ACTT, the Association of Cinematograph, Television and allied Technicians. The trade union was concerned about the lack of real public accountability on the part of the broadcasting organisations.

> The machinery of public trusteeship is invalidated if the trustees operate in secrecy . . . Lip service is paid to public service broadcasting; we do not see how this can be effectively instituted unless all decisions taken on Society's behalf are open to public scrutiny. Similarly, decisions affecting the present and future prospects of workers in television must be fully revealed to the Unions concerned. This should apply to BBC Governors' meetings, BBC and ITV accounts, Independent Television Authority franchise allocations, the proceedings of advisory bodies and all Government and company policy decisions relating to broadcasting.

That this feeling was not confined to a trade union with a leftish reputation is demonstrated by the comments of a Select Committee on Nationalised Industries reporting to Parliament also in 1972.

> The Authority [IBA] should study the methods of greater public accountability adopted by other countries, notably Canada, including their method of holding public hearings when inviting applications for or when renewing contracts. The Authority should also provide sufficiently precise information to permit the public to examine the criteria on which decisions are based on such matters as the particular regional structure chosen and the rentals charged. Prior to major policy decisions, the Authority should publish proposals and invite public debate.

Other suggestions being made in the Seventies included that there should be a National Broadcasting Council to keep broadcasting under review and to advise the minister responsible on national communications policy – a body which was felt to be urgently necessary in the light of the technological developments which were taking place with the development of new, more efficient cable systems. But another demand was for a different kind of Broadcasting Council, one on the lines of the Press Council to which an aggrieved member of the public might turn for redress if that person felt he or she had been misrepresented or otherwise unfairly treated. As has happened several times in the history of British broadcasting, the demands came from both Right and Left.

The grounds of the complaints were various. One was that if a member of the public or a professional working in television or radio felt they had been hard done by there was no independent body to which complaint could be made. MPs who favoured the setting-up of the Council were concerned by what they saw as the excesses of current affairs programmes. The professionals were worried that, if their work had been censored or otherwise suppressed or they had for unstated – presumably security –

reasons ceased to find employment, there was no court of appeal; the broadcasting authorities were judge and jury in the case. Reacting to the disquiet among MPs and to unfavourable editorial comment in the press (in which from the earliest days there has often been a current of antagonism to the BBC in particular) the BBC hastened in 1972 to set up a Complaints Commission and invited three elderly retired legal gentlemen to be its members; the BBC undertook to publish its adjudications in one of its journals and to 'pay proper regard to the views expressed in each adjudication'. It cannot be said that the Commission has left much of a mark on the public conscious-ness. The Commission's report for 1988/89 lists over 340 complaints – mostly concerned with scheduling and the boring nature of programmes. The Commission did, however, reprove both the BBC and LWT for cases of invasion of privacy.

Yet another proposal emanated from the Standing Committee on Broadcasting, which was composed of persons who worked in the media and had in many cases been active in advancing criticism of the regulatory bodies. It was that there should be a Broadcasting Commission responsible for overall executive control of broadcasting, managing the duopoly in the general interest of society. But others asked, even more radically, whether there had to be controlling bodies at all. There was no such control over the press or publishing. Ought not broad-casters to be seen as publishers and allowed to exercise this function restrained only by the law of the land which dealt with libel, slander and obscenity? Should the BBC not be financed by taxation – the aged and poor would pay less, the rich would pay more? (To the argument that this would mean government control came the rejoinder that the control was in fact there already, merely concealed in a very British manner.) Why were the Boards of Governors of the BBC and the IBA not more truly representative of the public – selected, for instance, by definable constituencies in society and responsible to them? That this last doubt was not just in the minds of radical critics emerges from the views of Bill Cotton, a former Managing Director of BBC

Television, who cheerfully admits to being a Conservative voter. He is discussing the situation as he found it at a somewhat later date under the Thatcher Government when the imbalance of opinion and interests had deteriorated.

> There was a problem which most of the Board accepted and that was that what you needed was some people who had different opinions to those of most of the people on the Board. Most of them thought the same way about most things. Not particularly good for public service broadcasting. And especially politically in a country where over half don't vote right of centre . . . You really need on the Board of Governors a proper representation of the 60 per cent of the people who have political views that are different from those currently held by the government of the day.

More worrying to the broadcasting institutions in the Sixties and Seventies were the complaints about the handling of current affairs, which came from both Labour and Conservative politicians and ministers. Some of the most trenchant criticisms came from Labour spokesmen who shared the view that television is too important a medium to be left to the broadcasters. One of these critics was Richard Crossman, the Labour politician and cabinet minister, who in the Granada Lecture of 1969 given in Guildhall expressed his concern at 'the trivialisation effect of television'.

> Where the trivialisation effect begins to work is when, on an important political issue – the long-awaited report of a select committee, for example; a controversial declaration of policy by a departmental minister; a Defence White Paper; the publication of an important Bill – after the news summary, whoever is in charge is given a five-minute interview in a magazine programme sandwiched between a couple of 'really entertaining' items . . . The fault, I suspect, lies in the first place with the producer who feels he must popularise what he regards as a dull, 'must' subject.

Questions about the Future: the Annan Committee

In the Seventies the Labour Government set up yet another committee under Lord Annan – it was traditional for the chairmen of such committees to be noble lords – to examine the future of broadcasting in Britain.

The Annan Committee made it clear in its report that it was well aware of the changes in the climate of opinion and of a new vision of life.

> [They] reflected divisions within society, divisions between classes, the generations and the sexes, between north and south, between the provinces and London, between the pragmatists and the ideologues . . . At once inflationary in the expectations of what political power could achieve and deflationary towards those in power who failed to give effect to their expectations, the new mood expressed itself in the rhetoric . . . of anxiety and indignation simultaneously utopian and sardonic. It was often hostile to authority as such; not merely authority as expressed in the traditional organs of State but towards those in any institution who were charged with its governance . . . It was during this shift in the nation's culture that the BBC began to recruit in sizeable numbers young production staff to man the second channel [BBC 2]; and inevitably the new recruits throughout broadcasting reflected these ideas in their programmes. The shift heightened the tensions between the Broadcasting Authorities and the young producers,

but even more dramatically between the Authorities and the Government.

The reason was that the programme-making of the new generation began 'to stir up resentment and hostility and protest against their political and social overtones'.

Perhaps it was awareness of this 'resentment and hostility' among politicians and important pressure groups that led the Annan Committee had doubts about the whole question of access, which it pronounced to be based on 'a formidable muddle'. This muddle it called on two philosophers to disentangle. Their answer was that while there is a right to speak in a democracy it does not follow that there is a right to be listened to.

> If I have a right to speak, you have an obligation not to stop me; but you do not have an obligation to listen to me. It does not follow that, because by a flick of the switch you can cut me off, I have a right of access to the medium, since there is a limited amount of time and air space.

The right of access, which was to continue to be an important point for discussion and eventually to be acknowledged as a legitimate demand, was therefore dismissed as 'unrealistic' since it could not be universally satisfied; which no one was seriously arguing.

A fourth channel

When the Committee began its deliberations, three channels were in use in that part of the wavelength spectrum available for television signals. In Britain they accommodated BBC1, BBC2 and ITV respectively. A fourth channel would soon become available. The Committee therefore had to decide how it should be used, to whom it should be allocated and how controlled and managed. The future of the channel has been the subject of considerable public debate and lobbying, one of the most interesting proposals being that the channel should be 'a publisher' subject only to the law of the land.

Among other proposals that had been put about was one from the advertisers represented by two important bodies, the Incorporated Society of British Advertisers (ISBA) and the Institute of Practitioners in Advertising (IPA). They wished to see two new bodies: a Public Service Authority and a Broadcasting Council.

The Public Service Authority would be financed by licence revenue and responsible for 'a national social and educational channel' using the fourth channel together with a national special interest channel run on the lines of BBC2. In other words, the two channels would serve only minority and cultural interests.

There would be a new body, a Broadcasting Council, which would be responsible for two 'general interest channels' – one of them in effect BBC1 financed by advertising and competing with the other, which would be a general commercial channel.

The advantages of the plan to advertisers were obvious; the new scheme would break the ITV monopoly on the advertising market – thus bringing down the cost of advertising on commercial television – and would at the same time allow programmes that were not mass audience pullers to be regulated to ghettos under the Public Service Authority. In the climate of the time their suggestion had little chance of finding favour; but it is interesting as an indication of the way two powerful lobbies (the ISBA and the IPA) were thinking – lobbies which would have the ear of the next Tory government.

Annan proposes

In the event the Committee, whose labours had cost over £300,000, made a number of proposals, some of which were radical, some practicable and others less so; but they did stimulate thought. In the list of recommendations that follows we have indicated – *yes* or *no* – those that were later followed

up by government or by the broadcasting organisations and
those that were not. The Committee recommended:

that an Open Broadcasting Authority be set up to run
the fourth channel (*no*);

that the channel should encourage productions which
said something new in new ways (*yes*);

that the new Authority should operate more as a
publisher of programmes and should not be in any
way responsible for their content (*no*);

that the BBC and ITV should be more willing to buy
programmes from independent producers and not
produce the bulk of their output in their own studios
with their own staff (*yes*);

that more time should be given to access programmes,
by which were meant programmes in which
individuals or groups would have the opportunity to
put forward their own views in their own way (if
necessary with professional help from the
broadcasters) (*yes*);

that broadcasting organisations should approach the Arts
Council to get help to finance the recording for
broadcasting – particularly on the fourth channel – of
some of the work of the major opera, ballet and
subsidised music and drama companies (*no*);

that the BBC and the ITV companies should set up a
single system for audience measurement and thus
eliminate the bickering over ratings produced by their
rival audience research units (*yes*);

that the IBA should be renamed the Regional Television
Authority (*no*) and run a single service of regional
television (*yes*);

that it should try to intervene less frequently in the
preparation of programmes (*yes*);

that the BBC should continue to be funded by the
licence fee but there should be concessions for
pensioners (*yes* and *no*);

that the BBC should continue to be what the Committee
(using the BBC's own favourite description of itself)

called 'the main national instrument of broadcasting'
(*no*).

The fate of the Report

The Report, which came out in 1977, was eventually noted and
approved (in a somewhat perfunctory way) in the last days of
Callaghan's Labour Government, which had other more pressing matters to consider. The cast of mind of the Committee did
not commend its report to the new Conservative Government,
wedded as it was to the concept of the market economy. Its
clearly stated view that 'an increase in the number of channels
does not necessarily lead to an increase in the range of
programme services which the viewer receives' did not chime
with the philosophy of the new Toryism any more than did the
remark that, if cable channels proliferate, the viewer is not
necessarily enriched even if the cable company is.

The Annan Report was a re-affirmation of the public service
ethos and, in retrospect, can be seen as marking the end of an era
when that ethos was part of the consensus. It repays attention
today because, as we shall see, some of its recommendations
surfaced in a very different context in the White Paper
published by the Thatcher Government in 1988 and entitled
Broadcasting in the '90s: Competition, Choice and Quality.

FIVE

The Fourth Channel

In 1980 the new Tory Government put through legislation in the form of a Broadcasting Act enabling the fourth television channel to start broadcasting.

That legislation did indeed set up the new channel as a publishing channel but not in the form proposed by the Annan Committee – that is to say, not as a publisher free of the control of any statutory body like the press or publishing, which are subject only to the law of the land on libel, obscenity, and breaches of the Official Secrets Act – and not under a new Open Broadcasting Authority. Instead it was placed in the care of the IBA, which – given its statutory duties – could not fail to have responsibility for the contents of the programmes. Even so, this was a remarkable and important break with the established pattern of British broadcasting.

It was accompanied by another important break with tradition. The channel's duties were defined as being limited to 'obtaining and assembling the necessary material' for broadcasting; which meant that it was not – unlike the BBC or the IBA and its ITV companies – to produce its own programmes, but would depend on independent producers. This change had been lobbied for, and was felt as a victory by, the Independent Programme Producers Association (IPPA), a lobby group formed in the late Seventies to campaign for precisely this kind of access to the television controlled – to quote the IPPA's director – by 'state licensed monopolies that have decided who will work for them and who won't'.

'Something new in new ways'

The Act laid three obligations on the Authority, which was technically and legally the broadcaster of Channel 4. They were:

to ensure that the channel's programmes contained a suitable proportion of matter calculated to appeal to tastes and interests not generally catered for by ITV;

to ensure that a suitable proportion of its programmes were of an educational nature;

to encourage innovation and experiment in the form and content of programmes;

to commission 'a substantial proportion' of its programmes from independent producers (as Annan had suggested).

These obligations then became the remit of the new channel. Its task was to 'say something new in new ways'.

Contrary to expectation, the Government did not fall in with the wishes of the advertising lobby, which was so vociferous and effective when the Television Act 1954 was being passed, and which now wished to see ITV's monopolistic power over advertising rates abolished by competition for advertising revenue from the new channel. Surprisingly, the resistance to the advertising lobby seems to have come from William Whitelaw, then Home Secretary in the Thatcher Government, who reportedly took the view that the advertisers would have to be disappointed because 'broadcasting was not determined primarily by their needs'.

Nor was the Government prepared to make a break with the tradition which has governed broadcasting in Britain from its earliest days; that this is a medium which has to be controlled in the public interest by a statutory body with a board of governors. Channel 4 was therefore placed under the care of the IBA.

While the legislation was going through Parliament a notable amendment was introduced and adopted. It established an entirely separate Welsh Fourth Channel which would carry all broadcasting in Welsh which up to now had been divided between HTV, the programme contractor for Wales, and the BBC. Strong and persistent pressure from Welsh nationalists – they included a threat from one prominent nationalist to fast to the death and a hold-up of a minister's car in the Welsh mountains – combined with a fear of alienating voters in Wales had paid off.

The Welsh Fourth Channel, Sianel Pedawar Cymru (S4C), was placed under the quite separate Welsh Fourth Channel Authority, which schedules around twenty-five hours of Welsh programming a week supplied in part by BBC Wales.

The passing of the Act was accompanied by a parliamentary debate that revealed some doubts on the Government's part about the financing of the new channel. This was to be by a subvention from the ITV companies. But if the companies' revenues were reduced by a large sum that would decrease the amount they paid by way of the levy. The Treasury would therefore be deprived of a considerable sum; which naturally did not please it or the Prime Minister.

The Channel 4 set-up

The IBA granted the franchise for the new channel, which – unlike ITV, which is regional – is a national one, to the Channel Four Television Company, a subsidiary of the Authority. It began to broadcast the new service in November 1982. It is financed by subscriptions from the programme companies that make up the ITV network; they in return have the right to sell advertising time on Channel 4 in their own franchise regions. S4C carries advertising, the revenue for which goes to HTV, the programme contractor with a franchise that includes Wales. S4C is also subsidised from the licence revenue of the BBC in that the Corporation provides some of its output but makes no charge for it.

Unlike the companies of the ITV network, Channel 4 does not have more than a minimal production capacity. It depends on independent producers and bought material; indeed, as the channel's Independent Producers' Terms of Trade states, it has the task of 'aiding the growth and sustaining the development of a secure and stable independent production sector in the UK'. It has therefore been instrumental in promoting a large number of production companies of varying sizes, of varying success and of varying life-spans.

The flow of offers to the new channel made it clear that there were many programme-makers who felt that it offered opportunities – given its remit to be original and innovatory – which were lacking where the BBC and the ITV companies were concerned. The nature of the new channel presented certain problems, which David Glencross, Director of Television at the IBA, describes.

> It was a very different channel from anything that had gone before because it was designed by Parliament to appeal to the interests that were not covered elsewhere on British television. But it wasn't a minority channel as such – and isn't a minority channel as such – since something like four out of five people tune in to it at some point every week these days. Nonetheless its share of audience of course approximates to that of BBC2 rather than either ITV or BBC1. And it did set itself, under the IBA's policy guidance, the task of trying to explore those kinds of programme interests, those kinds of programme styles, which were not by and large found elsewhere. That did, I think, lead it to test the frontiers of taste in a number of ways. It also led it to test the way matters of political controversy could be covered, because it had more hours at its disposal for factual programmes than a general channel. It had more opportunities to do documentaries and so it deliberately set out not only to have a one hour news at 7 o'clock but

also to provide greater opportunity than any other channel in Britain had ever done before for what might be called personal views – programmes with statements that came from a particular point of view – not necessarily from an individual, let's say from a group.

It tried quite deliberately to widen the role of access television. That was quite a change from the traditional style of British programming in which you either have balance within a single programme or you have a very very carefully structured short series in which one week there is this view and the next there is the counterview. Channel 4 attempted to widen that and this did cause difficulties for us because most of the people who wanted to take advantage of it were – generally speaking – on the left of the spectrum. And they rushed in, as it were, to fill the gap and there wasn't – at least initially – any really comparable input from the right. That problem was addressed after the first two or three years of Channel 4 and we have had a number of very interesting right-wing series as well as left-wing ones. I think that sort of balance over the whole output is an extremely healthy development in television.

Michael Grade, the present head of the channel, describes it as

the only channel in the country – the only channel out of four – which has a specific purpose and one very clearly laid down. And the specific purpose is to innovate, to fill in the gaps left by other channels. We have to keep that in our mind every time we commission a programme here and what we have to do for the audience . . . is to supply those tastes and interests that are not served properly on other channels.

He defines the audience for the channel as follows:

We are a national broadcaster – we reach 90 per cent of the population at some point. People who watch BBC1 or ITV watch Channel 4. We're different in the sense that what we are trying to achieve is to get viewers not to sit down and watch Channel 4 from 6 o'clock to closedown. We want people to pick and choose – to cherry-pick their way through the Channel 4 schedule. If you're running a major channel you're trying to get people to switch to your channel and stay there all evening. We don't want that because the chances are that the programme that follows is going to be of no interest to you but would be of interest to somebody else. So we have a different philosophy.

The audience for Le Piat d'Or

Michael Grade's views on the nature of Channel 4's audience are interesting for two reasons. One is that, unlike his counterparts in the BBC or ITV, he does not aim to establish channel loyalty and retain his audience all the time his channel is on the air; he accepts that they will come and go according to their interest in what he has to offer them. The second is that, although he rightly points to an audience of 90 per cent of the population for certain programmes, his account of the Channel 4 viewership can be taken as pointing to the possibility of a breakdown – a splintering – of the mass audiences. As a result both broadcasters and advertisers must reassess the viability of smaller audiences.

When the channel started, its audiences were dismissed as being marginal, near that lower limit of 250,000 viewers (a quarter of a million has long been regarded in the ratings war as a derisory figure) at which the ratings barely register. But there has come recognition from those hard-headed operators, the advertising agencies, that a small audience, if it is reasonably homogeneous and can be readily defined in terms of social class and spending power, is a worthwhile one. The audience for many of Channel 4's programmes are said to be in the higher social categories (as defined by income) and are therefore likely to be interested in expensive perfumes, expensive cars, and holiday villas in Spain, and to accept commercials in French or German. One does not see too many commercials for sliced bread or baked beans on Channel 4. The targeting of discrete audiences in this way is a new phenomenon in television advertising and is another, different and important, way in which the channel is innovative.

For the first time in British broadcasting the new channel opened up opportunities for a substantial number of independent film- and programme-makers as part of a policy which had important and positive implications for both television and the film industry. As a result, David Rose, the Commissioning Editor for Drama, can point to the fact that the channel receives something like 2,000 scripts a year.

> Many of these 2,000 are simply not worth a great deal of consideration . . . But the independent sector give us a huge opening because in British broadcasting – almost without exception – drama in the form of films had never been released in the cinema . . . So we were able to say to film-makers 'Come to us – if we like your projects we will be happy for them to be seen and distributed as widely as possible throughout the world' . . . Here was an opportunity for us to be partners in the production of films . . . So we have built up a new relationship, a partnership with the cinema industry which I think is well overdue.

Other new directions concerned the organisational structure of the channel. When it began to function under its first head, Jeremy Isaacs, he very laudably wished to avoid the large bureaucracies which have been characteristic of both the BBC and the large ITV companies (who, of course, require large staffs for their in-house productions). It has therefore operated with a small number of what are called commissioning editors who are responsible for their own areas of programming: documentaries, current affairs, drama, entertainment. Liz Forgan, the channel's director of programmes, recalls that 'once upon a time – when we started we could fit the entire editorial staff of the channel round a tiny round table'.

There was another crucial difference from the other channels which was that Channel 4 had a minimal studio capacity. Indeed

The Right to Reply, of which Liz Forgan was the originator is, as she says, 'the only programme we ever made ourselves inside this building. In those days it was very pioneering – now the television screens are full of them – but it was a real programme for viewers to criticise television and hold producers and executives responsible for things they didn't like.'

The organisation has grown since then – necessarily so, for in the early days, when the channel attracted programme offers and programme ideas, solicited and unsolicited, from a vast number of people (witness the 2,000 scripts), offers which had to be sifted through, there were complaints that the clearance of ideas took an unconscionable time. Speaking today, in an atmosphere where competition is likely to sharpen, Michael Grade admits that, 'in the past the channel has tended to give people definite maybe's which have lasted for two or three years – there are projects sitting around still waiting with producers still waiting for an answer. That's just unacceptable in a competitive situation.'

But whatever opportunities have been provided by Channel 4 there is a feeling – which is not merely a case of sour grapes – among some independent producers that something in the nature of a commissioning mafia is at work in the channel, that too much depends on being part of a network, of having the right connections.

Other criticisms of the channel's functioning have been concerned with the question of regulation (or censorship). Coming as it does under the IBA's regulatory powers, the channel could not escape the kinds of control exercised by that authority over the ITV network. Hence anxieties over that most difficult of domestic topics – events in Northern Ireland – which led to the suppression of a programme and to the retreat from an idea embarked on in the early days to have an alternative news programme called *The Friday Alternative*. This was a venture doomed from the start because alternative news must mean news based on a different perception of society and what goes on in it than that which informs the newscasts to which viewers, politicians, and guardians of the public weal are accustomed. It will therefore be seen as unbalanced, biased, and not in conformity with the impartiality which is laid down in the Television Act. It is noticeable, too, that the series *Union World* has not been continued.

Innovation – 'an easy word'

One of the requirements laid upon the new channel was to find new ways of saying things, to encourage 'experiment in form and content'. If this means new ways of using the medium, there is little sign of any formal experiment. The norms that govern the vast bulk of the channel's output are those of dominant television practice as it has evolved in the hands of professionals who are not always prepared to contemplate deviations from it. Experiment – seen as 'unprofessional' – tends to be confined to late-night programmes carefully segregated from the mainstream programmes. The debate about whether new things can be said without new forms has been largely abandoned.

It is naturally not an easy task to innovate either in form or in content, as Liz Forgan makes clear.

Innovation is an easy enough word, but it is very hard to institutionalise. When we started it was very easy – we just put up a brass plate and said 'if you've never succeeded in getting your programme on to television come and tell us about it' and there was a remarkable expectation that in among the rush of people who came with ideas some would be genuinely innovative. And indeed they were. We set up a different way of making television, a different relationship between the institution and producers. That in itself was innovative. We had some innovative ideas ourselves. But now all the independent producers have acquired offices and potted plants and responsibilities and they're more interested in volume of production and through-put and servicing their overheads than they are in having marvellous,

innovative ideas, which are very high risk ideas. Innovation is a very risky thing because the chance of getting
commissioned is pretty slim. So the independent producers are tending to get more conservative as they've got
more adult responsibility. Commissioning editors get a bit
more conservative because they've just settled back into
their jobs. And it's quite a difficult business to keep on
injecting something into the flow that makes sure you're
made uncomfortable enough to keep some innovation in
the mix.

The independents

One of the paradoxes of Channel 4 is that while on the one hand
it is seen by some politicians (of whom the Prime Minister is
rumoured to be one) as a radical channel, it has, on the other,
promoted by its commissioning policy the mushrooming of
production companies. Many of these are genuinely independent companies founded to pursue a particular line of
programme-making such as current affairs, a soap opera, a late-
night discussion programme. An analysis of the British television industry 'The Economics of Television' prepared by the
London Centre for Information and Communication Policy
Studies states of Channel 4's output for one year (1985) that
fourteen companies accounted for 54 per cent of the 690 hours of
new programming. 'The picture that emerges is of nearly three
hundred companies contributing a little over an hour of
programming each.' The organisational changes within
Channel 4, the report states, have led 'Channel 4's commissioning editors (responsible for various categories of programming)
to become executive producers and the Channel 4 cost
accountants (whose numbers have swelled and power increased)
to become the effective producers'. This means, say the authors
of the report, that in this structure the independent producers
become effectively employees of the channel, except that they
enjoy no long-term security or benefits.

Some of the 'independent' companies are likely in future to be off-shoots of the ITV contractors. Others are the result of 'sweetheart' deals in which a producer will, for instance, leave the BBC or a television company and become 'independent' with a promise of what is in fact continuing employment. In others still, some of yesterday's radical programme-makers and film-makers are constructing models of Thatcherite economics, standing on their own feet, fighting for survival. Some of those with the potted plants described by Liz Forgan are doing extremely well out of the channel and, to judge by the cost of their productions and their lavish style, are not exactly models of economical management. Naturally some of these companies are very short-lived – many indeed exist only for one production; other production companies act as facility houses for independent producers, providing office space, a telephone for the term of the production and secretarial help as well as acting as cost accountants and negotiating with the finance officers of the channel. What some people foresee is that, following the normal rules of capitalist development, the successful small companies will be taken over by larger ones so that within a relatively short space of time the channel may well be served by something like half-a-dozen production houses. It would be surprising if some of the survivors were not among the 'independent' companies which have been set up by some of the ITV contractors.

An important part in encouraging a different kind of independent production has been played by Channel 4 by contributing to base-line funding for and commissioning programmes from a network of workshops, facilities centres and studios up and down the country to provide access to ethnic minority groups, regional communities and the disabled. These projects are also supported by the British Film Institute, the Regional Arts Associations and the Local Authorities. Crucial to their success was the support of the technicians' trade union, ACTT, which has set up special flexible agreements to accommodate these enterprises.

A complaints commission

One other provision of the Broadcasting Act 1980 requires mention. It calls for the setting-up of a Complaints Commission 'to consider and adjudicate upon complaints of unjust or unfair treatment in broadcasts as well as cases of unwarranted infringement of privacy'. This legislation was obviously inspired by the feeling, mentioned above, that some body was required independent of the broadcasting authorities to which members of the public might present their grievances.

The Commission, whose hearings – following a bad old tradition – are held in private, does not consider complaints on the depiction of sex and violence, bad language, anything under the heading of 'taste' and 'standards', programme scheduling, or a programme not yet broadcast. Such matters, says a Commission leaflet, are at present for the broadcasting bodies themselves to consider.

There do not appear to be a vast number of complaints. Thus in 1986/87 the Commission dealt only with thirteen complaints against the BBC, mostly concerned with alleged misreporting. Four were rejected, two were upheld, and the remainder upheld to varying extents. In all but one case the BBC was instructed – as the Commission can demand – to broadcast the ruling and to print it in *Radio Times*. It is important to note that the Commission has no powers to lay down codes of conduct; it can merely find whether in its view the complaint is well-based.

If the Complaints Commission has not handled a vast number of customers, that is precisely because it does not deal with those matters which most exercise the viewers. Thus in the same year over two thousand complaints were addressed to the IBA. The largest number were about scheduling – the timing, sequence and availability of programmes. Then came taste and decency, followed by impartiality. Violence came below that. Perhaps the British public is less puritanical than the authorities think.

SIX

New Technology and a New Climate

With the advent of the Thatcher Government a change took place in the language and concepts deployed in the discussion of broadcasting. This was a government which saw clearly that a revolution was taking place in the way information is gathered, and disseminated – one that was based on extraordinary developments in technology. Wilson, as Labour prime minister some years before, had also been aware of the possibility of far-reaching changes and spoke of exploiting 'the white heat of technology'; but successive Labour Governments had done little about it. The new Conservative Government was committed to radical change; what distinguished it from its predecessors and marked a shift in the whole approach to broadcasting was that stress was now laid on the economic structure and functioning of the system, which was seen as an adjunct to the electronics industry rather than as an important social and cultural medium.

What speedily became clear as the Government got into its stride and began to turn its attention to the communications industry was that the terms in which broadcasting's future were being discussed were neither those of the radicals of the Sixties nor those of the liberal supporters of public service broadcasting who had produced the Annan Report. They had been concerned with social issues and social responsibilities, with cultural policies. Now the accent was on the development of technology because of the opportunities it offered to manufacturers and other entrepreneurs, to replace some of Britain's traditional industries, which the Thatcherite policies were decimating, to open up new markets, to export equipment and know-how. The medium was important because it could generate profits; the message it carried was not the first or even a major consideration.

The revolution in information technology, which was to play such a large part in the Government's thinking about the future of broadcasting, was bound up with the development of the microchip. Chips are pieces of silicon about a quarter of an inch square and are more accurately called 'integrated circuit packages' (ICs). Their name derives from the fact that they pack into a single tiny physical object the functions of a whole range of circuit components – transistors, capacitors, resistors. They are fed with electrical power, can receive signals from other chips, and can pass their output to other chips in the equipment they serve. This interchange of information is carried out through thin wire circuits printed on to a fibreglass circuit board. Different chips perform different functions. The construction of the electronic equipment is simply a case of arranging them in the proper order on the circuit board; it is a process that lends itself to mass production by labour that need not be highly skilled and is frequently female. In this it is typical of the new industries that have replaced the old forms of manufacture, which were labour-intensive – that labour in the key industries being often male – and highly unionised.

The use of chips allowed the building of electronic equipment without bulky wire circuits and made miniaturisation of that equipment possible. (One only has to recall the bulk of the radiograms which were still being manufactured in the Sixties with the compact sound systems of today to appreciate the changes their use brought about.) Microchips were not only small. They were also capable of handling and storing huge quantities of information with great speed. They were the essential components in computers, in space-craft, and in satellites which could be launched into space and kept in station there for collecting and disseminating information to government agencies (including the military and secret services), to large corporations, to television stations. Their use soon made the inclusion in television newscasts of live pictures beamed across the world a commonplace that merited no particular mention; they had become a routine event.

In 1980, early in the life of the Government, the Home Office commissioned a study of direct broadcasting by satellite (DBS), which was a relatively uncontentious subject since developments were at an early stage and the new services that satellites would provide did not seem an imminent threat to the established interests in broadcasting.

Direct broadcasting by satellite is possible because a satellite launched to a spot in space – to be exact, a spot some 36,000 kilometres or about 22,000 miles away from the Earth and directly above the equator – will revolve at exactly the same speed as our planet and thus appear to be stationary in relation to it. It is therefore called a geostationary satellite. It can be used to receive signals from a ground station and then transmit them directly to a small receiving antenna or dish which can be either in the viewer's home or at what is called a community reception point. The expression has connotations of good works but in fact means a receiving installation and distribution centre owned by an operator who distributes the signals, which can either be in clear or encrypted (scrambled). In the latter case the viewer requires a special gadget to obtain an intelligible image on the screen.

Satellites, which are operated by solar power, have a limited life-span of about seven years. They then have to be replaced. There is also the possibility that they may go out of service because of some malfunction. Unless there were a standby that would mean an interruption in the service and a wait of some time till a replacement was launched by rocket. It is therefore generally accepted that a direct broadcasting service requires to have three satellites available: one in station above the equator, with a spare in orbit and a third in reserve on Earth.

Had satellites existed in the early days of television they would have obviated the need for a network of transmitters scattered over the countryside, for complete national coverage can be achieved by a single satellite transmitter which lays a 'footprint' on a particular part of the Earth's surface. The footprint may be within national boundaries, but in Europe, where national territories can be small, there is likely to be a certain amount of overspill across frontiers – a signal aimed at Britain might be available in northern France. On the other hand, the satellite may intentionally lay down a signal that crosses national borders, one aimed at a public, and a market, in more than one country.

Signals from some twenty-five satellites can be picked up in Britain. Each satellite transmits several television channels of which almost a dozen are English-language ones. The earliest satellites using English were not based in Britain but in Europe. Because they were relatively low powered they required a large receiving disc, 1.5 metres in diameter, which made them unsuitable for individual households. Cable operators, who have been these satellites' main customers, require even bigger dishes if they want to pass a good signal on to their subscribers. Even then reception can be interfered with by heavy rain or snow.

A wet report

The Home Office report on DBS when it emerged was not radical in tone. Indeed it was rather 'wet' by Thatcherite standards; but the Home Office, as we have seen and shall see again, has a reputation for being soft on some issues. What was striking was its endorsement of the principle of public service broadcasting, which it noted 'is nationally and internationally respected' for the quality of the service it provides. It stressed the importance of diminishing the risks inherent in competition for audiences, since 'this can lead to a reduction in the range and quality of programmes'. It returned to this point, saying that

DBS was certainly a means of increasing broadcasting outlets but warned that an increase in the number of television channels did not in itself necessarily increase the range and quality of programmes; indeed, 'it can, if accompanied by all-out competition, reduce real choice'. Competition had been a feature of British broadcasting for more than a quarter of a century, but it had been regulated.

This is old-fashioned stuff, but the authors of the report also recognised that DBS offers important industrial and commercial opportunities, both at home and abroad, for the British aerospace and electronic industries, not forgetting the television rental industry. It therefore suggested a modest start towards a satellite launch.

The cautious note is struck again when considering the services that should be made available by DBS. They would require to be new and attractive, the report observed, if the public was to be persuaded to acquire the necessary receiving equipment. It conceded that it might not be possible to insist on the rules on balance and wide range which applied to public service broadcasting. These, it accurately noted, had their origin in an age when broadcasting outlets were scarce. But the way must not simply be opened to services consisting only or mainly of the most popular programmes. DBS should therefore generally be required to adhere to the programme standards of the BBC and IBA. There would, therefore, be a need for a public authority to appoint the programme providers; this body, the committee tended to think, should be the IBA. (And so in due course it was.)

On the financial side the committee saw possible problems. DBS would require an initial capital outlay of between £75 and £160 million. This could, in theory, come from private sources or from Government; but the Government was committed to reducing public expenditure. Indeed, the Home Secretary later confirmed in Parliament that the Government expected the capital cost of the satellite system to be borne by the private sector; it would be 'the first privately financed satellite in

Europe', he announced proudly. As for revenue, that would come either from advertising or from subscription – a method of paying for television new to Britain and still untested.

The report's approach to broadcasting harked back to Annan and beyond that to Reith. It lacked passionate commitment to market forces; it was paternalistic; it accepted in general lines the ethos of public service broadcasting. It was to be the last report inspired by these characteristics. Later reports would be more in tune with the economic, social and political aim of Thatcherism.

Cable and cable systems

Cable has long played an important role in transmitting signals sent by telephone, telegraph or telex, or in linking radio and television studios to transmitters. The cables used have traditionally been bulky copper cables; they can now be replaced by optical fibre cables, which consist of hair-like glass threads through which information is disseminated by laser beams. These cables are less bulky and easier to lay than the older copper wire cables. They are also able to carry a very large number of signals simultaneously.

Cable as a private system providing an adjunct to broadcasting was developed to distribute radio programmes so as to provide a better signal in certain areas which the BBC transmitters did not serve well – usually for geographical reasons such as that they were in the 'shadow' of a hill. It was a method of distribution that was economically viable only in highly populated centres, since it depended for its revenue on the rentals that people paid for the use of special receivers plugged into a cable system buried in the street outside. In the post-war years it was extended to distribute television signals, the operators being obliged to carry the BBC and ITV programmes whatever else they might transmit. But it did not flourish greatly. The reason was that both the BBC and the IBA saw to it that few places were not able to receive a clear signal through the air. The concept of public service broadcasting required a universal signal to be available to all licence-holders. BBC coverage is available to over 99 per cent of the population; if the IBA has been less zealous it is because some sparsely populated areas are of little interest to a commercial broadcasting enterprise dependent on advertising.

Because of the excellence of the television signal, Britain was behind other countries in the development of cable systems. In the United States, for instance, where the signal has been notoriously poor in many places, cable is highly developed in big conurbations. It was also popular in certain European countries like Holland where 65 per cent of TV homes are linked to cable; in Belgium and Denmark the figures are 64 and 50 per cent respectively. This is because none of these countries has a broadcasting system capable of producing large quantities of expensive entertainment; local television provides mostly a service of domestic news and comment and some home-produced shows. Much television viewing is of programmes produced by richer television stations and brought across the national frontiers by entrepreneurs. Such cable systems are obvious candidates to receive satellite television and to disseminate it to subscribers.

Cable enthusiasts then and now

It is a historical paradox that left-wing radicals in the utopian Sixties proclaimed the communications revolution based on the microchip, the satellite and the optical fibre cable, with much the same fervour as today's cable operators. Radical enthusiasts saw cable as a means not only for chores like delivering newspapers and mail by facsimile but for providing people – like the elderly and disabled – whom modern society had isolated from human contact with the ability to communicate with each other, to do shopping or deal with banks and other agencies from home. There was also the possibility in what would later be defined as the era of post-Fordism of certain kinds of work becoming decentralised as employees left their offices and went to work at home using computers and cable networks. It was a vision that had a touch of William Morris about it.

In a wider sphere it would, they maintained, provide a more open communications system by taking television (and radio) out of the hands of the great institutions and restoring it to the people. It would allow an interactive television system which would give viewers the possibility to answer back, to partake in a dialogue, insert their own material, make their own choices of programmes, construct their own schedules. In short, they would no longer be passive viewers. Others pointed to cable's capabilities as a means of communication within a community – but what is a community? sceptics asked – dealing with local issues, local politics, local activities, leading to greater civic awareness and involvement. And indeed there are interesting examples in the United States and Canada of cable systems run by citizen committees which strive to discharge that function with some success.

The promoters of cable in Thatcherite Britain share some of this vision. They wish to see the establishment of a broadband communication network – that is to say, one that can carry not only a large number of television signals but high quality stereo sound, two-way traffic in sound and vision and high speed data. Where television is concerned it will, they say, provide an almost unlimited number of channels and better quality pictures, and act as a distributor of national and international channels. It will also allow cable subscribers to do home shopping from video catalogues, book holidays on the basis of video films, view properties for sale, call up information from 'a remote video-disc encyclopaedia'. Cable, they add, can also be used for downloading electronic games to the consumer, for security alarms, panic buttons and other emergency services.

What critics of this vision find disturbing is that it could lead to a further atomisation of society, decrease human contact, further undermine the sense of belonging to a social group, reinforce that negative concept of individualism which is at the heart of Thatcher's political philosophy.

The real problem of cable, however, was the cost of installing it. A major expansion of cable systems in the UK would require expenditure on a large scale. The cost of providing a cable service to a medium-sized community or 100,000 souls or so would be in the range of £200–300 per house. It follows that to provide access to a modern cable system to half the homes in this country – those in the big conurbations – would cost something in the region of £2,500 million – admittedly, spread over a number of years. It is not a cheerful outlook.

Widening choice?

The government committee on cable was the Hunt Committee. Its terms of reference came from the Home Secretary, who was now (in 1982) the minister responsible for broadcasting. The Committee was to consider the question of cable in the light of the Government's desire to secure the benefits which cable technology can offer while safeguarding public service broadcasting.

The Report duly said that cable should be supplementary to public service broadcasting and that it was 'all about widening the viewers' choice' – choice being one of the shibboleths of the Government. There was no reason the Committee could see why there should not be a high standard of privately financed cable. They had a vision of a time when the whole country would be cabled. Then, because of the immense choice of channels, the cable operators would be free to act as publishers, restrained only by the law of the land. Until that utopia was achieved, however, they would have to obey certain 'liberal ground rules', observing impartiality and being careful to avoid offences against good taste and decency etc. It followed that there should be some supervisory body to regulate cable and grant franchises.

A lighter touch

So far the Hunt Report seemed – apart from its vision of the future – to be treading traditional paths. But its recommendations showed that the ground rules were being modified, that a new attitude to broadcasting (of which cable was a part) was emerging. Thus when it came to regulation of cable systems they favoured what would come to be called 'a lighter touch'. So there would be no requirement regarding range of programmes and balance. Adult films could be shown at any hour because of the availability of electronic locking devices to prevent children from seeing them (as if that would long deter today's electronically expert children). There would be no minimum quota of British material. There should be no limit 'in the early years' to the amount of advertising. Impartiality 'on individual channels' need not be required. Oversight should be reactive – checking that certain ground rules were observed, but not attempting constant supervision of the service.

There was, of course, a regulatory body to hand in the shape of the IBA, which was critical of the Hunt Report on the grounds that its proposals put at risk the principles of range and quality of programmes; that unrestricted advertising would undermine the revenue of Independent Broadcasting; and that the unlimited imports of cheap foreign programmes would lower programme standards, jeopardise employment and undermine British production. The siphoning away of programme material by cable operators would actually decrease choice, particularly in rural areas. Regulation was clearly necessary, in which case the IBA proposed itself as the regulatory body, being well qualified on the grounds of its experience in handling franchising, programme oversight, advertising control and technical standards. Moreover, were it to be given the function, unnecessary duplication and increased public expense would be avoided. But the IBA did not get the job, which went in 1984 to the Cable Authority.

The Committee might wish to 'provide encouragement to new multi-channel operators' but there was a rub: the Committee's deliberations took place against a present-day reality that was not cheering. The role of cable in Britain was still very limited. (Today – in 1989 – one and a half million homes are 'passed' by cable; only just over a quarter of a million are actually connected.) As the IBA was quick to point out, cable channels would probably be limited for the foreseeable future to less than 50 per cent of the population.

The history of cable companies in Britain points to a lack of interest by the public. There had been, it was true, a short-lived pay-television experiment in London and Sheffield based on a coin-in-a-slot meter, the system known as 'pay-as-you-view'. Six community television stations had opened up in various parts of the country, but only one was still in operation. Nor did it look as if anyone was prepared to embark on the immensely costly business of laying the wide-band national network that would make the vision of cable come true or even of providing large-scale cable installations for the great conurbations.

The new tough approach

Meanwhile Mrs Thatcher – perhaps as an antidote to the canny reports produced for the Home Office – had appointed advisors on information technology (IT) and created an IT Unit in the Cabinet Office. Its report on cable systems published in 1982 was very different in tone and approach, less 'wet', more truly Thatcherite, as might have been expected of a unit located so close to the centre of power and decision-making.

The Unit's report stated bluntly that the prospects for existing commercial cable systems were 'bleak' unless the present regulatory controls on programming, such as the duty to carry BBC and ITV programmes, were lifted.

It was significant of the new thinking that the arguments advanced for the encouragement of cable had little to do with cultural interests (in the widest sense, i.e. including entertainment, sport, etc.) or social uses. Cable should be supported primarily for economic and industrial reasons. There was, said the Unit's report, a fast-growing market in consumer and business electronics, which offered the possibility in the long term of extensive cable links between homes and businesses. The direct markets for equipment could total £3,000 million or more. There would be a stimulus to overseas sales of programme material, information services and cable expertise. If no action were taken, the Unit warned, there would be adverse effects on the balance of payments.

Cable, the report concluded, was 'an essential component of future communications systems', and offered great opportunities for new forms of entrepreneurial activity. But, while that was the long-term potential, in the short term cable would depend on an audience that wanted entertainment. A cynical reading of this conclusion is that the people would be encouraged to subscribe to and therefore fund a cable system with the promise of better programmes and more variety, only for it to be exploited – once it was developed – by business and commercial interests.

The Unit saw no reason why cable systems should necessarily lead to unsuitable programme material or to a reduction in the range and quality of service on the public broadcasting networks which would be competing for audiences. Indeed the broadcasting authorities would benefit from the opportunity to exploit existing programme material – in other words, the chance to sell to the cable operators programmes that had already been transmitted, and therefore hardly a great attraction – or from the possibility of creating new programmes. The BBC in particular, they asserted, would stand to gain, but they did not explain why this should be so.

The Unit did, however, sound one important warning note. Unless by mid-1982 the Government had announced its policy on cable systems, laying down technical standards and defining the relaxed controls on programmes, there was little hope of a modern cable industry being established in Britain.

How much real hope did they have of this proposal, which would have large financial consequences, being implemented? On the face of it, it was unlikely that a government which was then and has continued to be notoriously unwilling to indulge in public expenditure on such essential items in the nation's infrastructure as school and hospital buildings, sewers, roads and railways, would undertake to cable Britain. Nor was it likely that private investors would do so.

The Cable Authority's view

In 1984, two years after the report appeared, the Cable Authority was set up. It has the task, firstly, of franchising and licensing cable systems, or more strictly the provision of broadcasting-type services over cable systems, and secondly of regulating the content of these services in terms of taste and decency, violence, advertising control and so on.

Jon Davey, the Director General of the Authority, takes a positive view of the situation.

> We have a growing technology which is capable of delivering however many channels you want, particularly as we progress over the next few years from coaxial cable to optical fibre . . . Cable has the capacity that no other medium has, and moreover it has the capacity for two-way transfer of information in a way that none of the other broadcasting technologies do have . . . Although other technologies are coming along, the value of cable, the need for cable is going to be strengthened. If one looks at the long term future, I find it very difficult to conceive of a country that will not be more or less fully cabled.

In the meantime, he admits, there is the problem in that, as the figures of homes connected show, people have been slow to hook up with the present cable systems. This he believes can be attributed to a cultural barrier which he thinks is coming down fast.

> People in this country have been so used to broadcasting services provided without payment other than the standard licence fee, which everybody's always had to pay, that the idea of buying more television has been an

alien one. Therefore people have tended to be slow to catch on, as after all they had been slow to take up any new media development . . . If you look at the pattern of take-up on all these things it starts off slowly in the early years and then the curve climbs rapidly. I think that is what we're going to see in cable.

But how many people actually use cable?

The number of subscribers to cable systems – we're talking about the people who are receiving from cable something other than ordinary broadcast television – is 268 thousand. Most of them are actually connected to old cable systems . . . the kind of cable systems that were first installed back in the 1950s and 1960s before the television transmitter network was fully developed. If you look just at the numbers of subscribers to the new broadband franchises [i.e. ones capable of carrying a large number of services] that are being installed under licence from the Cable Authority it's only – out of those 268 thousand subscribers – about 53 thousand subscribers. That is a figure that is going up steadily – in fact over the last quarter that figure went up even though the number of subscribers to the old system fell over the three month period. At the moment we have only ten cable franchises operating so those 53 thousand are spread across the ten areas. Over the next few months we should have a number of others also starting to operate; so as the number of systems grows and each system grows throughout its area, I think the expansion is going to be quite substantial.

It is a rather modest forecast. So far 52 franchises have been granted between 1983 and 1989; of these only about a dozen are actually in business. A number are still looking for finance and backers. There have been threats from the Authority that it will cancel franchises if the sluggards do not show progress. One interesting development has been the arrival of American cable interests working through Jersey companies. Their hopes – and the hopes of the Authority – must be bound up with the development of satellite broadcasting. Cable seems to some to be the answer to distributing satellite signals in heavily populated areas. The agreement whereby Robert Maxwell has contracted to distribute over his cable system the programmes of Sky Television, owned by his arch-rival Rupert Murdoch, is a sign of possible future developments.

SEVEN

The Omega File – Thinking the Unthinkable

One of the bodies which acted as an unofficial but influential think-tank for the new government was the Adam Smith Institute, which in 1984 produced a publication on communications policy called *The Omega File* – a title which brings up according to one's taste images of science fiction, Cold War adventure or Biblical apocalypse. Like all think-tanks, the Institute was prepared to think unconventional thoughts and to propose extreme solutions; it was not said that the Government would adopt all its proposals. They are worth looking at, however, because the terms the Institute employs and the assumptions that underlie its arguments are consonant with the fundamental political philosophy of the new Toryism. And they were to surface in other more official contexts.

The report is of extreme interest because of its clarity and brutal frankness; it feels free to carry the policy of not mincing words even further than the Information Technology Unit, presumably because, not being an official body, it can have fewer inhibitions.

The free market

The new note is struck at once in the opening pages of the report when the authors are discussing access to the spectrum of wavelengths suitable for communications. Here, instead of talking of privileged access to a scarce public resource with accompanying social duties, the proposal is that parts of the spectrum should be sold or leased by auction rather like fishing rights on a salmon river. This is followed up by the assertion that 'consumer choice and the optimization of opportunities for innovation are best served . . . by the establishment of a free market'. Only sale or lease of frequencies will make the users aware of 'the true value of the resource they are using'. (This is the principle on which the local authorities charge a fee to visit the crater of Vesuvius.)

What the report welcomes in the new technology is first and foremost the 'unrepeatable' (a word appropriately culled from the vocabulary of high-pressure salesmen) opportunity to break out of 'the straitjacket of the broadcasting duopoly'. Cable, for example, will free the viewers and transfer decision-making – that is, the choice of programmes – away from those who 'know what is good for them'. The accompanying increase in transmissions will inevitably bring higher quality television and communications to more and more people. The cry that a free market system will threaten quality they dismiss as the slogan used 'throughout history' of the monopolist wishing to preserve his (*sic*) privileged position.

But there is a problem; it is that Britain is 'not exactly in the forefront of cable usage'. (This is putting it mildly since the figures quoted in the report show the percentage of TV households with cable to be only 14 per cent, as opposed to 55 per cent in the Netherlands.) Moreover, it seems that a cable system relying on television only is unlikely to be viable: only other – mainly business – uses, it admits, will ensure economic success. What is more, the cost of installing cable is high. Given the high cost, the authors argue that strict technical standards – such as the requirement to put cable underground or that the whole franchise area should be wired – could be 'the last straw'. They therefore are in favour of an overhead cable, if necessary, 'between gardens'. They are unworried by the thought that some potential customers might be left out, for 'it is better for half an area to receive cable because it is profitable' than for no

one to do so. The same argument applies to rural areas. Cable
television is a luxury; it follows that there can be no logical case
for urban taxpayers to subsidise the rural viewer. (Cross-
subsidisation, as in the case of rural buses and rural railway
lines, is anathema to thoroughgoing free marketeers.) In any
case, 'those who enjoy the benefits of rural life cannot necessarily expect urban dwellers to carry the costs for them'.

What they find regrettable is that government policy is
contradictory. On the one hand there is 'a strong will' to allow
private development of cable and to promote change; on the
other, there is a strong paternalistic lobby, backed by a
protectionist one – the ITV networks – who are attempting to
preserve the status quo and to impose 'regulatory burdens' on
the cable industry. This paradox, as they rightly call it, reflects
that contradiction within the Conservative Party which emerged
at the birth of commercial television and which has reappeared
over a number of social issues – health, water privatisation – and
does not appear to have been resolved. It is a split which can be
defined in various ways as between Wets and Dries, the Tory
grandees and the New Men, the landed interest and the City, the
One Nation Tories and the Free Marketeers, the true
Thatcherites and those who hanker after some sort of consensus
on matters of public policy.

The authors of the *Omega File* are unreservedly free
marketeers with the courage of their convictions. It is always,
they say, far better to have independent market regulation by
competitive pressure than political regulation through a government agency. It follows that cable ought to be treated like any
other branch of publishing. By extension there is no point in
placing restrictions on the ownership of channels by political
parties and religious organisations. And political parties should
be able (as in the United States, they might have said) to buy
cable time or even purchase their own station.

Omega and the sovereignty of the viewer

It is when the Adam Smith Institute's thinkers come to deal with radio and television that one begins to detect, even more strongly, that blend of radical populism and consumerism which is the hallmark of Thatcherite policy. Rightly describing the television licence as an annual tax, the report criticises it not on the grounds of social injustice – that it falls, like the poll tax, equally heavily on the poor and the rich and has to be paid in a lump sum – but for the more metaphysical reason that there is no relationship between the viewers' satisfaction and the revenue the BBC receives from the licence fee. Conversely, advertising is preferable to the licence fee as a method of funding broadcasting precisely because what advertisers have to pay is 'directly related to viewing figures via programme popularity'; which may make economic sense in a free market but elevates the cost per thousand into the key concept of broadcasting philosophy.

They find the present system to be seriously flawed since the BBC is guaranteed a stable income 'almost regardless of the quality or content of its broadcasting'; furthermore, the licence fee grants the consumer no sovereignty, 'since the price of viewing is not related to the consumption of the product'. This line of thought leads naturally to the view that a better system is to be found in Pay TV, which charges the viewer directly for each programme watched, by a slot-meter or some other form of billing. But this method has not been tried out in Britain – at least where broadcasting is concerned – and the report has some (justified) doubts about how the British public would react to it.

Of one thing the report is sure. British television must move to meet the demands of its audience (but how do they know what these demands are and how do they differ from what is on offer?); which will only happen, they argue, if the licence fee is abandoned. There can be little future for a system, the report says threateningly, which discriminates against the paying viewer in favour of the decisions of a bureaucrat.

Turning to the question of whether the public service duopoly should continue, the report attacks the pessimistic view that quality must inevitably be affected by increased competition. It points to the success of the newspaper industry in 'informing, educating and entertaining' as evidence of the benefits of competition. Since the total supply of all kinds of programmes will inevitably increase, so too will the number of quality programmes. This optimistic faith in exponential growth has, however, to be considered alongside the report's candid admission that the average quality of programmes will decline – a decline, it believes, that will be offset by the benefits of an expanding market. Here the authors draw a historical parallel. Broadcasting, in their view, is at the same point of development as was book publishing when it was overtaken by that other technological revolution: the invention in the fifteenth century of the printing press. True, the quality fell as a result of an increase in the number of titles; but to compensate for this there was Shakespeare (who, to judge by the history of his texts, however, seems to have been conservative in his attitudes and not at all keen on being published).

What particularly incenses the authors of the report is what they see as the elitist argument in favour of quality. They have a vision of a small number of mandarins passing judgement on what is and what is not a 'good' programme. They are forced to admit, however, that these mandarin judgements coincide 'from time to time' with those of the audience. Their own attitude is a straightforwardly populist one: 'the only fair criterion for judging a programme is how many people watch it'. It follows that ratings are the final arbiter of success and quality.

A new deregulated model

It is not surprising that when the report comes to consider the structures of broadcasting it comes out in favour of deregulation. One regulation that should be relaxed is the control of commercials at present exercised by the IBA under a code of advertising. To allow the ITV network to compete with cable and satellite there should be fewer restrictions on the advertising of cigarettes, betting and other products or services which are at present forbidden. Limitations on the amount of advertising should be greatly relaxed and even completely removed.

But it is when the authors of the report come to make proposals for the future organisation of broadcasting that they are at their most root-and-branch. To stimulate 'the competitiveness and public responsiveness' of BBC TV:

1. BBC1 and BBC Breakfast Time should be financed by advertising;
2. BBC2 should depend on a mixture of advertising, sponsorship and subsidy from the remainder of BBC TV;
3. BBC TV News should be a separate body funded by a levy on all three BBC services and fees from other subscribers like cable or satellite companies. This, they argue, would maintain the integrity of the BBC News Services to which they pay tribute as having a worldwide reputation for quality;
4. BBC Radio would also be remodelled;
5. Radios 1 and 2 would be hived off and financed by advertising;
6. Radios 3 and 4 would depend on advertising or sponsorship and subscription on the lines of the Public Broadcasting System (PBS) in the United States, which is partly funded from Federal sources, partly from sponsorship and partly from donations from viewers (the Report describes it somewhat inaccurately as 'successful' whereas it has notoriously considerable financial problems);
7. BBC local radio stations would be made completely independent and sold to the highest bidder;
8. The IBA should be replaced by a 'body more akin to the Federal Communications Commission in the USA' (which has a very light touch indeed). This new body would become a commercially-aware licensing

body and be less concerned with control and restrictions. It should shake off the notion of public service broadcasting and encourage competition.

More comments

The importance of these suggestions was not that the Government was necessarily going to adopt them wholesale. It is the useful function of such unofficial bodies as the Adam Smith Institute to put ideas into circulation where they will be picked up in editorials, discussed favourably and unfavourably by politicians and others, read by civil servants, and thus influence proposals and suggestions from other more authoritative and official bodies. Some of their ideas – such as auction by tender, the hiving-off of BBC Radios 1 and 2, the demotion of the IBA from its position as a powerful regulatory body – seem (to put it in minimal terms) to have struck a chord in the minds of those officials and politicians who drafted the White Paper published four years later in 1988 and called *Broadcasting in the '90s.*

What is striking is the animosity displayed by the authors of the report towards the idea of public service broadcasting and the populist scorn with which it is dismissed. The attack is launched, as we have seen, from a position that uncritically embraces commercialism and market forces, making numbers the sole criterion of quality. They resent what they see as the power of an elite which makes the final decisions about what the public may watch; what they do not confront is the fact that in the commercial business of providing and scheduling broadcast material – whether for cable, satellite or terrestrial television – decisions about the kind of programmes to be made, their cost, their target audiences and whether it is profitable to transmit them, will depend on the views of a restricted number of executives. They, too, are an elite operating on criteria very different from those of public service.

Nor are those who make these planning decisions under the present system arrogant in their approach to their task, as is shown by Michael Grade, the head of Channel 4.

> The truth is you never know what an audience wants – you make a professional guess, which can be informed by research on past experience. I believe that the one thing likely to produce a programme that the public doesn't want is predictive research. That is a certain route to disaster. You rely entirely on the creative flair of individuals. And we stand or fall on our ability to pick talent, to spot talent and give it backing to produce programmes that they want to produce. The only successful programmes you ever see on television anywhere in the world – and that includes America – are the programmes that come out of some lunatic's obsession with a particular idea and their ability to carry it out.

The comparison between the unregulated broadcasting output of the future and the entertainment and information provided by the popular press will not be found universally convincing, given the record of some of the popular press, which is coincidentally owned by magnates who have already moved into broadcasting where – given deregulation – they would no doubt pursue the same policies. Nor is there any evidence that an increase in the number of down-market popular papers breeds variety; on the contrary, they resemble each other more and more in their coverage and presentation.

The argument about viewer sovereignty is an old one and the report adds little to it. No one with any experience of working in or for the BBC or the ITV network can possibly think that there is a lack of contact with the public: that contact takes place daily through letters and phone-calls, through a complicated system of advisory committees of varying usefulness and through

audience research with its sampling techniques and apprecia-
tion indexes which register viewer satisfaction – the same
marketing techniques on which the sellers of goods and services
rely for information about their customers' wishes. But to give
the devil his due, it is impossible not to agree with the report's
view that local radio stations serving ethnic and other cultural
minorities should be allowed to broadcast in the big conurbations – as indeed some of them now are. But, as we shall see,
the Government, which embodies the aspirations of the Adam
Smith Institute, at first pulled back from recognising them
because of difficulties of control; which means that it was afraid
that they might – politically speaking – fall into the wrong
hands.

The merit of the Omega report is that it is not mealy-
mouthed, that it calls a bulldozer a bulldozer and a demolition
job a demolition job and makes manifest trends of thought –
especially economic thought – which were in the following
years to be a sub-text to the debate on broadcasting. There is a
sense in which no one who follows these matters should have
been surprised at the tone of the Omega report. They would
have seen from the United States the consequences that
logically flow from the application in a thoroughgoing way of
unregulated market forces to broadcasting. They had been
spelt out by no less a person than the chairman of the Federal
Communications Commission in the United States, who –
surprisingly, given his official duties – called for the replacement of the trusteeship model for which he was responsible
(there were those on both sides of the Atlantic who thought the
trusteeship he exercised was somewhat lax) by the market-
place approach.

> Communications policy should be directed towards
> maximising the services the public desires. Instead of
> defining public demand and categories of programming
> to serve this demand, the commission should rely on the
> broadcasters' ability to determine the wants of their
> audiences through the normal mechanisms of the

market-place. The public's interest then defines the public interest.

It looked as if Britain was catching up with Reaganonomics.

EIGHT

The New Realism

The economics of broadcasting came increasingly to engage attention in the Seventies and early Eighties. The reasons were not far to seek. The BBC was experiencing growing financial difficulties. It also had problems on the political front where it was seen as being too unresponsive to government desires, too arrogant, presuming too much on its prerogative as the originator of public service broadcasting; these problems were solved by appointing to the Board of Governors what were, from the Government's point of view, reliable figures, and sacking the Director General. Many people found it significant that the new incumbent of this post had come from industry and rose up not from the programme or editorial side of the Corporation but from the accountancy department, having been Chief Accountant, BBC Television. This attitude was in part an expression of straight-forward cultural snobbery; in part of surprise at a reversal of the long-standing BBC tradition that the Director General should be above all the organisation's editor-in-chief and that all other branches served the programme departments. But the appointment was also a pointer to the difficult position in which the BBC found itself: this was that, because of inflation, the costs of making programmes and running the organisation were mounting more quickly than the licence fee – which politicians have traditionally been loath to increase lest they become unpopular with their voters – could be expected to rise. There was therefore strong reason for a look at the BBC's finances.

It is true that the Annan Committee had wondered whether the licence fee was really the best way of financing the BBC, and had considered a number of alternatives – such as direct taxation, advertising and sponsorship – only to conclude that the licence fee should be retained. It made, however, no serious attempt at an analysis of the economics of the broadcasting duopoly; it was not a task for which the Committee was particularly equipped. The BBC, drawing on long experience of dealing with government inquiries, seems to have presented itself as whiter than white and told the Committee that the licence fee was a unique success. In the end the Committee believed them; but it is indicative of a certain doubt in the Committee's mind that the Report asks the question: 'Is all this rhetoric?'

The Peacock Committee

'Yes' was the answer given by a committee set up by the Home Secretary in 1985 'to undertake an inquiry into possible ways of financing the BBC' – an undertaking which inevitably involved examination of the financing of its competitors present and future: commercial television, cable and DBS. The chairman appointed by the Government was Professor Alan Peacock, a liberal economist – liberal in the sense that he does not favour state intervention or coercion in economic matters – who was also vice-chancellor of Britain's only private enterprise university.

His appointment aroused considerable alarm among what might be called the cultural and social lobby made up of professionals, academics, and trade unionists. But some voices on the Left welcomed the possibility of a thoroughgoing look at the broadcasting institutions from a new angle. James Curran, an authoritative academic on the Left, felt there was a danger of their being 'corralled reluctantly into support for the status quo'. In this they paradoxically found an echo on the Right of the political spectrum, for both Left and Right were persuaded that the BBC was in need of a shake-up.

This had various grounds. There was the feeling that the consensual view of broadcastable opinion – the concept of a 'mainstream' to which the BBC had so long adhered – worked to exclude voices on both the Right and the Left of the political spectrum. There was a suspicion that the BBC was too large, too dominant in the field of broadcasting, too monolithic, and that the public might be better served by a variety of broadcasting institutions. There was resentment (again from both ends of the political spectrum) at the BBC's assumption of authority; at the way, for example, in which it placed its stamp of approval on a particular definition of culture – one that was being increasingly questioned by those who saw a continuum from high culture to low or popular culture. There were complaints from the Left at the BBC's lack of accountability, the extreme secrecy that attended its decision-making. (For example, members of the General Advisory Council, which is presumed to represent the public, were forbidden to make public what went on at its meetings.) On the Right, there was a feeling that the Corporation was too sheltered from market forces. Where both camps agreed was in favouring a break-up of the BBC, the Right wishing to see a number of competing bodies and the Left a number of public service bodies dealing with television, radio and local radio. The fact was that the BBC had contrived to alienate considerable and important sections of the public. In this situation an examination of the Corporation and its finances by someone who had not until now been heard to express an opinion publicly on broadcasting policy might be no bad thing.

It was also true that some people on the Right who were in a position to know judged that the committee was by way of being a punitive expedition against the BBC. One of them was Lord Rees-Mogg, formerly Editor of *The Times*, who from 1981 to 1986 was Vice-Chairman of the BBC where he was, in his own words, 'basically an unpopular governor'.

I was unpopular with pretty well everybody including certainly many of the BBC broadcasters because I was in

conflict with the attitudes and atmosphere of the BBC –
particularly during the period when Alasdair Milne was
Director General. I thought that the producer regime at the
BBC at that time was moving away from the traditional
standard of the BBC in respect of impartiality, was showing
a kind of assertion of arrogance towards the rest of the
community which in the end was not going to be acceptable. What was going to happen was that the politicians
would get fed up with the BBC behaving in this way and
would start to cut it down to size. And indeed they did. The
Peacock committee was set up with just such a view.

The Peacock Committee was to be of great importance, for, as
the Conservative Home Secretary said of it, it set the agenda for
the future consideration of broadcasting.

The Committee at once struck a new note, which if it was less
strident than that of the Omega report, was equally determined
in its application of the market philosophy and market models to
broadcasting. The concept of the viewer was to be replaced by
that of the customer or consumer who chooses television
products in a market. This view of broadcasting as a market, the
Committee was aware, 'is much more willingly accepted in the
USA than in Britain'. It was clear that the Committee intended
to apply a version of the market economy (which might differ
from the American model) to British broadcasting and thereby
to call the whole system into question. This they proceeded to
do in spite of the fact that, in the course of visits abroad, the
Committee's members were faced in almost every country with
'expressions of amazement – even from NBC and ABC [two of
the big networks] in the United States – that the British should
be thinking of changing their system, which is almost universally admired'. So what was wrong with it?

The consumer in chains?

The Peacock approach is succinctly stated in a chapter from the
Committee's report headed: The General Problems of Broad-

casting Finance. Here, starting from the unexceptionable proposition that 'it is a good general principle that any service to the public should be designed to promote its satisfaction', it goes on to declare that 'the public are best served if able to buy the amount of the service required [by them] from suppliers who compete through price and quality' (provided certain conditions are fulfilled). The accent is therefore to be on freedom for members of society defined as consumers.

The first of the necessary conditions for a good service 'requires acceptance of the proposition that the consumer is the best judge of his/her own interests'. The stimulus of competition brings benefits to the customer because it provides the supplier with the incentive to offer new and improved services. Broadcasting, the Committee states, is no exception to this rule. The second condition for the operation of a free market, which is the Committee's basic model, is that the goods or services should be priced. Applied to broadcasting, this condition logically leads the Committee to think that the system of broadcasting finance in Britain requires to be changed, for – although it is possible to know the cost of producing programme categories – the broadcasters attach no price-tag to their products. But without a price-tag, goes the argument, how can there be real choice?

Those viewers who opt to watch the BBC have no idea what programmes are costing them; they have no direct financial link with the supplier of the television services. In a sense, under the licence system, one BBC programme is as dear or as cheap as any other. What the report is getting at is the fact that the consumers or customers in this case can only express their dissatisfaction by switching off their sets or switching channels; which may affect the BBC's ratings but not its pocket. Pressure from customers for more programmes or programmes of better quality can, the Committee remarks, at best be exercised indirectly through the various advisory bodies of the BBC, by using the complaints procedure, by lobbying members of Parliament and so on. They are therefore largely powerless. Peacock is intent on endowing them with muscle. Were a price to be attached to programmes then the volume of sales would, as in any other open market, provide 'a low cost method for the exchange of information between consumers and suppliers'; the latter would quickly learn of changes in consumer preferences while the former (given – and it is a big proviso – a large choice of channels) would be able to shop around.

The cosy duopoly

Until that age of abundance arrives we are left with 'the cosy duopoly' of the BBC and the IBA, which had been the target of the Omega report. The Peacock Committee, too, has it firmly in its sights. What it finds unacceptable in the duopoly arises from the economic fact that where only two firms supply a product and both are roughly of the same size, they are likely to find it to be in their common interest to avoid competition and to come to an understanding about the division of the market and an agreement about prices. This arrangement has operated between the BBC and the ITV companies over the prices paid for bought-in programmes and old films. Dog has not normally eaten dog. The consumer is then faced with what is in effect a monopolistic situation even though the two suppliers may occasionally quarrel over the division of the spoils and may not be able to prevent, at least in the longer run, the entry of competitors into the system. If the incentives normally provided by competition are lacking there is a strong assumption – there certainly was in the Committee's mind – that programme and transmission costs will be higher than necessary. Moreover, innovations in methods of programme production and in programme content will not be a condition for financial survival.

The programme companies of the ITV network enjoy under the duopoly a situation whereby competition is excluded and advertising slots are rationed. Economists (there were two on the Peacock Committee) would expect that in these circumstances exceptional profits would be earned. (They were not mistaken in their expectation.) This had the unfortunate consequence that it was possible for managements, while keeping the shareholders happy, to share out the monopoly profits between management and employees. (That this has been the case is clear to anyone who has worked in the system from the extremely advantageous terms which the unions were able to agree with the companies individually and locally or nationally and collectively through the Independent Television Companies Association (ITCA).) Nor was this all. The broadcasting industry, it was submitted to the committee, was wasteful of resources because of over-manning and self-indulgent work practices.

Nor was this all. Since 1974 the levy imposed on the companies has been no longer exacted from their revenue but from the profits arising from their domestic activities – i.e. excluding overseas sales of programmes. It is not, therefore, in the interest of the companies to cut costs. Cost cutting would simply increase profits and these 'excess profits' would be skimmed off by the levy. Padding has the opposite effect of cutting profits and, from the Treasury's point of view, of giving a disappointingly low yield. This casts a new light on Mrs Thatcher's recent attack on the television unions as the last stronghold of trade union power in the economy, a view which is disputed by the Chairman of Thames Television.

> Governments don't understand very much about broadcasting and its finances. The Prime Minister a bit over a year ago described ITV as 'the last bastion of union restricted practices'. It was at a seminar she held in Downing Street to which she kindly asked me . . . I said to her afterwards that she was out of date. The Monopolies Commission review of ITV practices has found none other than in the areas – which we know, and are concerned about – of the talent unions: that is the actors and the musicians. In terms of keeping down our production overheads all the companies have made very considerable progress. No question that four or five years

ago the Prime Minister's remark would have been quite valid.

This view has been substantiated by the report submitted to the Government by the Monopolies and Mergers Commission. The fact that it was asked to examine restrictive trade union practices in the television industry seemed to many to be an extraordinary extension of its remit. The report was eventually released with a minimum of publicity and contradicted Mrs Thatcher's belief that malpractices flourished in both the BBC and the ITV companies.

What genuinely astonishes the Committee is that British broadcasting was deliberately created as a duopoly subject to extensive government regulation. It has to concede, however, that this regulation is a necessary evil to protect the interests of viewers and listeners so long as the consumers of broadcasting services do not and cannot express their preferences through direct payment and are, into the bargain, offered a limited range of services. Unfortunately, government regulation inevitably means that the financing of broadcasting becomes highly politicised – a state of affairs which, as a liberal economist, Peacock deplores. Such problems do not arise with commercial television since it does not rely on the licence fee for funding. In its case the consumers (while they may have to pay the licence fee as citizens) are not directly involved in the pricing policies of the ITV network, which can be regarded as 'selling audiences to advertisers' (while naturally having to provide programmes that attract viewers in the first place). The problem here, as the Committee sees it, is that the advertising slots are limited by the IBA and therefore scarce and that ITV takes advantage of this fact, and of its market position as the only commercial channel, to hold advertisers to ransom.

One feature of broadcasting financing as we at present know it is that regulation, by insisting, for instance, on minority and regional programmes, produces what the report calls 'cross-subsidisation'; thus in the case of the BBC there may be no close relation between the licence revenue from a given area (as might be Central Scotland) and the cost of regional programmes to that area. But 'cross-subsidisation', as the National Board for Prices and Incomes had noted with some surprise back in 1970, also occurs in the ITV network: Channel 4 is an obvious case, for the ITV companies must pay a sizeable proportion of their advertising revenue as a subscription to fund the channel. Thus inexpensive programmes or programmes with high ratings and high advertising rates subsidise low audience or expensive programmes. This the report sees as a flaw in the system.

The duopoly has other features which the Committee finds displeasing. They state, for example, that 'satisfaction of the consumer is not the driving force behind the activities of the producers' who are accused of devoting a good deal of their effort to enhancing their reputation with fellow professionals. Here no doubt the Committee had in mind the various Eurovision contests, the BAFTA awards and other prize-giving ceremonies which are annually celebrated on the air in programmes that depend for their interest (which is small) on a parade of show business personalities and presenters. (But what, one might ask, about those Young Business Man/Woman of the Year awards, not to mention the banners of the Queen's awards?)

The BBC and the scissors effect

One of the problems faced by the BBC, as we have seen, is that the revenue the licence fee produces is constantly threatened by inflation. At the same time the report recognises that the BBC has to try to keep in step with the ITV companies' spending power in the sense that the Corporation must strive (not always successfully, it has to be said – witness the strikes by BBC staff over pay – to offer broadly comparable salaries to staff in order to prevent a loss of talent and expertise. But whereas the licence fee is subject to negotiation with government, the ITV's income derives from advertising which rises with growth in the gross national product. There is therefore an increasing gap between the income of the BBC and that of the companies which can only be met by economies. As the BBC put it to the Committee, maintaining its spending power in relation to the ITV companies was its biggest headache. The result has been that under the twin pressures of inflation and competition the BBC has been forced at frequent intervals to ask government for an increase in the licence fee – a process which (although the report does not spell it out) has long been suspected of providing government with the opportunity to put pressures on the Corporation, which can expect that a government will prove difficult if it is unhappy with the BBC's editorial policies. The Committee therefore asked the BBC to consider whether the licence fee should not be linked to the retail price index. The BBC assented to this suggestion (which has since been put into practice) provided the licence was properly protected and (significantly) 'distanced from the political arena'.

Alternatives to the licence?

Taxation?

In its search for an alternative to the licence fee, which it found in some real sense immoral, the Committee examined the possibility of financing the BBC from taxation, of which the Labour Party at that time was in favour on the grounds that television is more universally used than most other public services such as health or education and should therefore be funded in this way. But this would raise the old question of government control and pressures. (There are those who believe that this would at least be an honest system since, as an ex-director general wrote, the BBC is 'a powerful and efficient instrument which has all the appearance of independence, but which, by the existing provision of the charter and licence, [the Government] can control at will'.) It even considered – only to dismiss the thought – funding by a national lottery, and might have recalled (but did not) that, faced by large-scale licence defaults, Italian television at one time used to run a successful lottery on the serial numbers of licences.

Advertising?

That left advertising and sponsorship which, given its bias in favour of commercial competition, the Committee might have been expected to favour and to suggest as a source of funding not only for all television channels but for BBC Radio as well. But they were scrupulously honest in their researches and found that 'in general the greater the amount of advertising the narrower the range of programmes'. The report cites the example of Canadian English-language television which rarely buys British programmes for prime-time scheduling because 'few advertisers will buy spots alongside them', the reason being that British drama is seen as unpredictable and abrasive. (The blandness of American television derives from the same sort of judgement; programmes must not upset possible consumers of the product being advertised, who might then switch off or switch channels.)

From the USA, too, came evidence of the influence of advertisers – for instance, on casting. Since advertising agencies are particularly interested in urban women aged 18 to 49, especially affluent ones, it is important to cast men with sex appeal. The word is that women want 'men with their shirts off'. Curiously the Committee did not discuss examples of the fate of programmes – *The Beverley Hill-Billies* was one example – which have been killed off not because they were unpopular but because the viewers were too old or too young and therefore had not sufficient purchasing power to satisfy the advertisers. (In more recent times, since the Committee reported, there is evidence that British advertisers are dissatisfied with ITV not because it does not have a large audience but because that audience is too down-market, too working-class and too elderly – in short, has not sufficient spare cash to buy the products advertised.) The Committee sums the situation up by saying that in an advertising-supported system 'there is no reason why the value of programmes to advertisers should correspond to the value that viewers and listeners attach to them'.

Having considered the evidence, the Committee concluded that if both the BBC and the ITV companies, in a duopoly situation, were competing for advertising revenue, they would do so by constructing their schedules so as to maximise audiences at peak times and probably at most other times as well. Controversial programmes, critical consumer programmes, current affairs programmes and satire – in short, anything challenging conventional attitudes – would not attract advertisers. A narrower range of programmes must be expected.

Sponsorship?

Sponsorship as a method of funding is most widely practised in the USA. The question for the Committee was: What influence did sponsors have on programme policies? There had, as we have seen, been grave worries about this in the Fifties when commercial television was first mooted. What the Committee discovered was that there was concern in America that sponsoring companies tend to favour safe programmes to the detriment of more experimental ones, although there was contrary evidence of sponsors using their influence positively in favour of adventurous (and therefore prestigious) programmes. What was clear to the Committee was that sponsors have a more direct interest in and influence on editorial judgements than normal advertisers. On the negative side the Committee quotes a famous example of how in 1958 the American Gas Association banned any mention of gas chambers in a programme about the Nazi period because of their negative associations which would rub off on to the product being advertised.

Subscription

Having dismissed all other alternatives to the licence fee, the Committee was left with subscription, which it embraced with enthusiasm, accompanying an exposition of its virtues with full-page colour diagrams. These are projections of future developments, the last of which envisages a situation in the next century when optical fibre cable will have replaced copper co-axial cables almost everywhere. These cables will carry to domestic and business consumers not only signals from DBS, cable and television but telephone messages, teletexts, telefax, data transmissions and video telephone services in varying combinations and permutations.

The virtue of subscription in the view of the Committee is that even before this utopia is realised, viewers and listeners will be able to pay for the ability to pick from a wider choice of programmes. The programmes would not, however, be available to everyone, for they would be encoded; consumers would then have to rent a decoder. This could be hired at a price that included a 'programming charge' by which the BBC would be financed. Then 'the insulation of the BBC from its customers and from market disciplines' would be ended. What was not clear, however, was how many people would be prepared to subscribe for the services; but, given a low weekly or annual charge, almost 80 per cent of those interviewed in a marketing exercise indicated that they might do so. But the figures, the Committee noted, were not very reliable. Nor was it certain (but the Committee does not say so) that the sums raised by subscription would finance the kind of output to which viewers have become accustomed from the BBC.

Subscription, then, was clearly what the Committee favoured as providing a market mechanism; but it considered that subcription presents certain problems. Thus it might discourage programmes for which there is not large demand but which can be defined as beneficial to viewers. Presumably the Committee had in mind programmes for cultural and other minorities or for social ends, e.g. to encourage adult literacy. Again, subscription, by giving viewers the freedom to opt out, might take away options by limiting the types of programme available. It might also try to optimise profits by charging high fees which would in effect exclude some customers and 'deny many households half the television channels they now enjoy'. Faced with this dilemma, the Committee surprisingly and feebly, given the strength of its convictions about the need for freedom from controls, falls back on government intervention to regulate prices and even the quality of service provided; but such regulation, it adds, would have its problems, which are precisely those it had wished to solve in a radical way. Nevertheless it was for subscription that the Committee settled.

NINE

What is Public Service? The Question Restated

Before coming to conclusions the Peacock Committee attempts a definition of public service broadcasting – a term which, it says, is widely used and has a reasonably clear meaning in common parlance. But the Committee wished to reach a concrete definition in its own terms.

The bedrock of public service broadcasting, as we have seen, is usually taken as being the ineluctable duty to inform, educate and entertain. But what else? The Committee examined various people on the subject but did not find them very enlightening. Interestingly enough, the BBC spokesmen, who might have been expected to be prime witnesses, proved unsatisfactory, either making very vague claims for public service or claiming too much. What did emerge from examination of professional broadcasters was an insistence on the principle of geographical universality – that is to say, that television and radio signals should reach as high a proportion of the population as possible. (BBC coverage reaches over 99 per cent of the population.) There seems to have been no mention of the normative function of broadcasting which bulked so large in the early Reithean definition, nor of the moral examples on which he insisted. What the BBC representatives seem to have conveyed was that a proper mix of programmes, including light entertainment as well as other forms, was an important consideration – which is a Reithean idea based on the view that 'exposure' to a mix of programmes can serve to enlarge the public's tastes.

What the Committee came up with as its own definition was one which disregarded social or cultural considerations, although such considerations are naturally implicit in it. It was admirably succinct: 'The best operational definition of public service is simply any major modification of purely commercial provision resulting from public policy.' In the best of all possible worlds, then, the role of public service will be minimal, for market forces will determine the provision of programmes, which will presumably be offered in abundance. What we have in the meantime, however, is a highly imperfect market.

The fundamental conclusion of the Committee was therefore that British broadcasting should move towards improving that situation and aim at creating 'a sophisticated market system based on consumer sovereignty'. Such a system has the advantage of recognising that viewers and listeners are the best judges of their own interests and that they can best satisfy them if they can purchase whatever broadcasting services they require from as many sources as possible. These are what the report defines as 'the important welfare benefits theoretically associated with a fully functioning market'.

The Committee is sceptical enough to assume, however, that consumer choice and market forces alone may not create a demand for certain categories of programmes roughly defined as purveying knowledge, culture, criticism and experiment; these might not be commercially viable from the point of view of the broadcasting entrepreneurs but might be considered socially or publicly desirable and therefore supported by the audience in their capacity as citizens and voters. From this flows the need for some statutory body financed by grants and with the remit to contract producers to provide programmes which discharge these civic and public services. But that body would not exercise censorious controls, since the law of the land already provides sufficient protection against breaches of decency, defamation, sedition, blasphemy and so on. If people were offended by what they saw on their screens or heard on their radios they should have recourse to the law.

A proper market

So the goal should be a market; but what would be the definition of a satisfactory market? The Committee defines it as follows:

1. full freedom of entry for programme-makers;
2. an indefinitely large number of programmes;
3. facilities for pay-per-programme or pay-per-channel;
4. differentiated charges for units of time.

What is required for the achievement of this state of affairs, a genuine market, with all the advantages the Committee believes it would bring, is a decision by 'policy makers' (presumably government) to encourage the technology required to wire Britain for cable – cable not only capable of distributing terrestrial and satellite television but of recording the consumption of programmes by individual viewers so as to make some sort of subscription possible. Till that day comes, the Committee admits, regulation will have to continue.

In line with Annan and the Omega report, the Committee foresees broadcasting becoming like the publishing industry. Just as people do not acquire everything that is published but buy or subscribe to what interests them, so the members of the television audience will make their choices from the multiplicity of channels. The Committee is hard-headed enough to recognise that average quality will decline and – significantly – reproduces in excuse, almost word for word and without attribution, the account given in the Omega report of the effects of the invention of the printing press which caused a huge expansion in publishing and a decline in quality but also gave us Shakespeare. But this proliferation of choice will take time to be achieved. The Committee foresees three stages of development:

1. in the first, satellite and cable will develop but most viewers will continue to patronise the BBC and ITV;
2. in the second there will be a proliferation of systems, channels and methods of payment leading to:

3. an indefinite number of channels with payment per programme or per service.

To which there is a rider: that there will be a continuing public service element throughout all three stages, providing special programmes for minorities, educational programmes, cultural programmes.

Peacock proposes: stage one

The proposals of the Peacock Committee follow logically from its attachment to the market and to deregulation, even if that goal lies some distance away in the future.

Typically the proposals begin on a very practical level. All new television sets should (not later than January 1988) be required to have a peritelevision socket and associated equipment to make it possible to receive and decode encrypted signals. But what reforms might be introduced in the meantime?

The BBC

We know that the Committee considered advertising an imperfect tool for providing a satisfactory market mechanism. It is therefore not surprising that the Committee recommended that the BBC should not be asked to accept advertising so long as the present organisation of broadcasting and its regulation persist. Its finances should, on the other hand, be secured against inflation by being index-linked to the Retail Price Index. The BBC should also be made responsible for collecting the licence fee, a service for which the Post Office at present charges it £60 million per annum (a figure which admittedly includes the costs of chasing up defaulters and dealing with complaints about reception and interference with BBC signals). Persons wholly dependent on a pension should be excused payment.

The Committee could not reach unanimous agreement on a

more radical proposal affecting BBC Radio, but a majority favoured the privatisation of Radios 1 and 2 and their financing by advertising. Linked to this proposal is another which is even more contentious. It is that any further radio frequencies that become available should be auctioned to the highest bidder. This is in fact the most radical of all its proposals for – as the Committee must have been aware – it marks a reversal of the view which has obtained up to now that certain public resources are the inalienable property of the public at large and that, while persons or organisations may be given privileged access to them, these resources remain public property. They are only to be leased, not bought outright. This suggestion again echoes the thinking of the Omega report and is certainly consonant with that of the present government on public resources (witness the privatisation of water). Competitive tender is a concept which the Committee extends to the franchise awards to ITV contractors. Were the IBA to award the franchise to some party other than the one making the highest bid, the Authority should be required to give 'a full, public and detailed' explanation of its decision – in other words, defend its disregard for the laws of the market and the sovereignty of wealth. It follows that DBS franchises should also be put out to competitive tender.

Independent production

As far as the production of programmes is concerned, the recommendation is that over a ten-year period both BBC and ITV should be required to increase the proportion of programmes supplied by independent producers to not less than 40 per cent of their total output. Here the motives are a complicated blend of the economic and the political. It was obvious that one result of this proposal (were it accepted) would be to accelerate the casualisation of the television industry; which would mean opportunities for some but at the same time save the broadcasting organisations as employers the burden of insurance, pensions, holiday pay and sick pay. These would devolve increasingly on individuals or on small production companies which would simply lay off staff during slack periods or 'holidays'. Looked at in the light of the fears expressed by politicians of the danger of 'producer power' – which were fears out of all proportion to the fancied danger – the drive towards increased use of independents can be seen as a way of weakening such power as producers do actually have; for if they have power at all it is because they have had an institutional base and a secure position from which to fight. A proliferation of freelances means that the power of the producers is undermined.

On the economic side the Committee had been persuaded that the broadcasting institutions have not been as careful to keep costs down as they ought – we have seen that the managements of the ITCA companies in particular were judged to have been sharing profits with the unions – and that independent producers are more cost effective. But the call for a very large increase in the employment of independents would also be in line with the political attack on trade union power, which has been a signal element in Thatcherite policies. The proposal is presented as a defence of free speech since the sapping of the union positions would remove the danger of the screens being blacked out (a very rare occurrence). It would also allow an attack on trade union restrictive practices (which are a way of protecting jobs and of restraining employers), for in small production units (often staffed by newcomers to the industry with no trade union background or consciousness) there may well be examples of corner-cutting in production – some logical and overdue, some designed to exploit labour more efficiently. The employment of independent producers would also foster the growth of small-scale units which would provide the economic basis for the broadcasting system of the future as envisaged by the Committee – and indeed, as we have seen, by Channel 4, which does, however, stress the need for it to be 'secure and stable'.

Channel 4

The Committee made one other important proposal. It was that Channel 4 should be given the option of selling its own advertising and no longer be funded by a subscription from the ITCA companies.

Stage two: subscription

Looking towards the second phase of the electronic revolution, the Committee states that a political decision will be required on the timing of the change-over to subscription. The decision will have to be made on the basis of the number of households possessing sets that can receive and unscramble the signals. Their rough guess, given the time it takes for sets to become obsolescent (just under ten years), is that this will not be before the late 1990s. But who should pay for the decoders which will be required to receive the broadcasts? Even though it estimates that they might be as cheap as £50 by that time, the committee argues – in a surprising moment of paternalism – that there is a good case for the BBC or Government either paying for the equipment or providing cheap finance. To excuse this lack of confidence in the market to make people buy the gear themselves they draw a curiously unconvincing economic parallel between investment in roads, which – they argue – facilitated trade, and investment by Government or a public service institution in decoders, which will promote trade in the broadcasting market. (But did Government in Britain actually finance road-building in the days of the industrial revolution or earlier?)

A public service body

The Committee's last thoughts – apart from a reiteration of the necessity of abolishing the licence fee – are for the need to protect in some way what cannot be much more than the rump of public service broadcasting: the service which will provide those programmes that 'the public recognise as being in their own interest' but are not expected by liberal economists to be willing to pay for. The Committee favours the setting-up of a Public Service Broadcasting Council responsible for the secure funding of Radios 3 and 4, local and regional radio and public service television programmes on any channel. Its funds should be drawn from as many sources as possible.

The final conclusion of the Peacock Report is that what is required is 'direct consumer choice rather than the continuation of the licence fee'.

Peacock pie

What is remarkable about the Peacock Report is that it addresses the question of broadcasting in terms just as radical as, but less crude than, those of the Omega report – terms that had not been employed by any previous government committee.

Reactions to the Peacock Report were predictable. On the one hand there was approval of the application of liberal economics to broadcasting, which was felt to be overdue and in tune with the Thatcherite policies as applied to other institutions of the Welfare State. On the other, there were voices that deplored the terms of the Report and its insistence on considering the audience as first and foremost consumers whereas they were also, and arguably more importantly, citizens whom the broadcasting institutions had a duty precisely to inform, educate and entertain, providing them, for example, with a public forum where politicians and other figures of power and authority may be cross-examined, social and local issues debated, and the opinions of members of the public given some space. The argument that there is a civic dimension to broadcasting had been put to the Committee, which described it very fairly as an expression of the view 'that even if consumers are freely-acting agents aware of what they are doing, they do not automatically choose the pattern of goods and services which is in their best interest. The argument carries the implication that, if this is true of broadcasting, the government must identify or have identified by some broadcasting authority the programmes which are in the best interests of the viewers.'

This argument, the Report comments, 'will clearly appeal to those who regard broadcasting as a public service designed to influence and not merely to reflect the public's preference for programmes'. It was one that the Committee rejected in line with its general refusal to contemplate state intervention even through an 'arm's-length' regulatory body. But it is a conviction that is still held firmly today. It is restated by Jonathan Powell, Controller of BBC1, in terms that raise the important question of television's (and radio's) role as the provider – within a public service system – of a public space where questions of importance to viewers as citizens, as social and political beings, are raised in the mainstream of programming, and not in the relative obscurity of special and minority slots.

> On BBC1 . . . documentaries and factual programmes, which have always been popular in this country, can be seen and get wide audiences in the middle of more obviously entertaining programmes and the range of people who watch television and watch the programmes, programme for programme, tends to be a broad cross-section of the country. It doesn't break down into those kinds of ABC1's and D's and E's advertisers like to talk about . . . And I think that is a valuable thing. If you believe that television has anything to contribute to culture then it seems to me that as a cultural force public service broadcasting – quality broadcasting of this kind – with all the kinds of restrictions and objectives that go with it, has actually meant that the wider community in this country has actually got some shared values one way or another and at least has something they can engage in a dialogue with, even within families.

On a purely practical level the suggestion that Radio 2 could somehow be detached from the rest of BBC Radio was surprising, for it seemed to show that the Committee had not understood how difficult – if not impossible – that move would be, given the way in which the BBC is organised with shared services serving more than one radio programme.

The proposal that the BBC and ITV should be required to employ a percentage of independent producers was probably inevitable and desirable.

The suggestion that Channel 4 should be made to sustain itself on its own advertising revenue without a subscription from the ITV contractors was rightly seen as an ominous threat which, if fulfilled, would compel Channel 4 to compete for revenue with the ITV companies.

Admittedly this was not a White Paper but a report on the financing of the BBC; while disturbing in its implications, its recommendations were not mandatory, might not be followed up by Government. But it was a powerful voice and its proposals went to join previous suggestions – which tended to favour a free market economy for broadcasting and to be inimical to or suspicious of the concept of public service as being economically and ideologically unsound.

An economic critique

There were few attempts to challenge the Report on economic grounds. One was a report prepared for the Greater London Council on behalf of the London Centre for Information and Communication Policy Studies based in the Polytechnic of Central London.

For the authors of this work the Peacock Committee had 'performed the valuable function of placing the economics of broadcasting firmly at the centre of the policy-making agenda'. It was therefore 'a healthy antidote to that bias in favour of cultural questions, divorced from and to the neglect of economic ones' – a bias shared by broadcasters themselves and by 'those members of the cultural elite who see it as their business to keep broadcasting policy free of what they see as the philistine influence of economic analysis'. But while they welcome the economic approach they are critical of Peacock's liberal economics, which rest upon certain arbitrary value assumptions, such as that 'individual freedom rather than optimized material welfare is the primary goal of policy and that any intervention by the State and any form of coercion is viewed with a priori suspicion'. Such a position will logically focus on the coercive nature of the licence fee rather than on its 'efficiency as a resource-allocating machine'. The licence is 'a contract between the government on behalf of the licence payers and the BBC to deliver a given service at a given price'; which, as they point out elsewhere in their report, is not high at 2p per hour for the BBC's service. (ITV works out slightly cheaper at 1.5p per hour.)

The authors start from a distinction between private goods, which are, by definition, in short supply and therefore rationed by price, and goods like TV programmes which are public goods in the sense that one person's consumption of them in no way diminishes anyone else's chance of watching them because they are not destroyed by the act of consumption. Broadcasting is, in fact, a process of instantaneous reproduction in which the marginal cost of each extra viewer or listener is zero to the producer. Normal goods are easily rationed by prices, but these conditions do not hold for the cultural industries and 'it would be inappropriate to map the model for the private commodity on to that of the cultural industries'.

The broadcasting industry is one in which novelty is a paramount requirement and risks are high. To deal with the peculiar nature of its product and the problems that arise in the context of the market, the industry has exploited economies not only of scale but of scope. Citing the French concept of *culture de flot* (flow culture) they believe that consumers will pay for the service, provided a high enough proportion of a stream of items is to their taste. 'From the point of view of economic strategies, the crucial matter is the range of material over which central editorial and financial control is exercised . . . Any restriction on the range of programmes (products) a broadcaster offers will damage its viability, for this is to restrict the choices from which a portfolio (of programmes) can be constructed.' In these circumstances, they go on to argue, the opportunities for balancing 'losses' by 'profits' become increasingly limited. And this is as true of audience figures (the broadcaster's reach) as it is of direct financial returns. Thus if the BBC were to be confined to a narrowly defined 'public service' ghetto, it would be forced to become increasingly cautious in its programming policy, even within that narrow range, and consumer choice would be severely restricted. The authors of the report note that in the USA specialist channel providers like Home Box Office (which supplies by subscription films and programmes not available on the three commercial networks) are being pushed towards the network programming model so as not to be confined to a narrow, uneconomic audience segment.

Discussing the problem of how to effect savings in an industry which (as all observers agree) has suffered from rising costs, they come to the conclusion that neither a fully competitive system nor the introduction of the profit motive solves the problem. Indeed competition is likely to raise the general level of costs. Certainly that has been the recent Italian experience where, as they point out, competition has increased the cost of bought-in programmes by as much as 1,000 per cent.

On the question of choice related to channel capacity and the argument that a competitive market structure will maximise audience choice, they identify financial constraints as a more powerful limitation on the real availability of broadcasting channels than spectrum availability. In any case, choice between competing channels is not necessarily, because of competitive scheduling, the same as diversity of programming.

Their conclusions are that all types of broadcasting finance are for one reason or another sub-optimal on strict economic criteria.

We are therefore choosing between inefficiencies on what

must be, of necessity, political grounds. If one has to choose between advertising and Pay-TV, the former optimizes total consumption, while the latter more efficiently realises consumer demand. From the point of view of optimizing consumption and matching price to marginal cost, the licence fee remains preferable to either and in the conditions of real channel scarcity a licence financed monopoly would be likely to optimize audience choice.

Will interventions like that of the Peacock Committee, they ask, enable Britain to take advantage of the growing market for TV programmes and at the same time maximise the diversity of opinion, information and entertainment available to the British consumers? It seems doubtful, they think, that that can be achieved by increased competition. Certainly to the authors of the Report the proposal that the BBC should be confined to a ghetto of 'serious' and 'minority' programmes – thus being prevented from maximising its economies of scale and scope – makes little sense. Indefensible on economic grounds, such a course would have to be argued on political grounds alone.

_____ TEN _____

The White Paper

Since the Thatcher Government came to power, broadcasting
(including cable) had been exhaustingly discussed unofficially
by the Adam Smith Institute, officially by the Information
Technology Unit set up by the Cabinet Office, and by two
committees – the Home Office Committee on cable and the
Peacock Committee on the finances of the BBC. All of these, as
we have seen, produced reports. There were also to hand the
results of an inquiry by the Home Affairs Committee – the
parliamentary select committee that overseas the activities of the
Home Office – into 'the implications for the regulation of direct
broadcasting by satellite and cable television, the future of
public service broadcasting in an increasingly deregulated
industry; and the potential of subscription as a means of
broadcasting finance'.

The Home Affairs Committee made over forty recommendations. Some of them are unexceptionable, such as that the
principles of public service broadcasting should be an integral
part of the broadcasting environment; that it is a prerequisite of
any new financial and institutional arrangements that the British
television industry can continue to sustain and develop its
programme-making capacity; or that all opportunities for
consumer choice should be investigated but not at the expense
of services currently received free of charge. But one contentious recommendation is that a system of regulated tendering
should be introduced when the ITV franchises are next due for

renewal in 1992. Their argument is as follows:

> There would be obvious advantages in introducing a
> more commercial element into the allocation of ITV
> franchises. The Exchequer would gain maximum
> revenue from the sale of frequency space . . . Tendering
> would also be a simple way of ensuring cost efficiency
> within the ITV companies.

There was therefore a mass of material to hand on which
ministers and their civil servants might draw when deciding
what steps should be taken to define the future of British
broadcasting.

It was becoming clear what some of the important issues
would be.

1. What is the future of the BBC? Should it remain
   intact?
2. What is the future of the licence fee?
3. Is subscription a possibility?
4. What is the future of the IBA in a climate that
   favours deregulation?
5. Should the IBA franchises be put up to tender and
   awarded to the highest bidder?
6. Should the ITV network continue unchanged or be
   faced by competition?
7. Should Channel 4 continue to be subsidised by a
   subscription from the ITV companies? Should it
   depend on its own advertising revenue?
8. What is the place of independent producers in an
   expanding industry?
9. What about programmes standards in general in a
   system given over to competition?

In spite of the amount of preliminary discussion it was some
time before the Thatcher Government got round to producing
legislative proposals for the future of broadcasting. A White
Paper was promised but kept being postponed. The speculation
was that either broadcasting had a low priority on the Government's agenda – governments tend to find broadcasting a

tiresome and contentious subject – or else there were differences of opinion between the Home Office, the custodian of broadcasting, where there were said to be patches of wet, and the bullish Department of Trade and Industry pressing for the freeing of the market forces.

During the period of waiting one step was taken which followed up Peacock's suggestion that the proportion of programmes produced by independent producers should be increased. In 1986 the Home Secretary announced that 25 per cent of the new programmes made for ITV and the BBC should be made by independents. In response to this move the BBC set up an Independent Planning Unit to deal with contracts and other matters and committed itself to reaching a figure of 500 hours of programming by the independent sector by 1990 with budgets allocated at £20 million. But what other of Peacock's suggestions would the Government take up?

'We must protect our young people'

In June 1988 Mrs Thatcher spoke to the Press Association and addressed herself to television and radio. (Rumour has it that – like most politicians – she sees little television but, being an early bird, is a devoted listener to the *Today* programme on Radio 4, which she has been known to ring up offering a contribution. Although she referred to 'the decisions we have taken' – a reference presumably to the proposals that were shortly to be put forward in a White Paper – she limited herself to generalities. Not surprisingly, she would 'welcome more television channels because I think that the free movement and expression of ideas is guaranteed far better by numbers and variety than it ever can be by charter and specific statutes'; which was a double swipe at the BBC and the IBA. Following the Omega report line she did not accept the argument, which she candidly stated she did not like, that a multiplicity of channels 'will drive television down market'. She had always believed that there was a market for the best and that 'the British public can be a lot more discriminating than that'. Significantly she mentioned subscriber channels as enabling us 'to have some very upmarket television', which many people would welcome.

Her speech did, however, reveal the contradiction which the Omega report had detected between faith in the market and a paternalist approach to regulation, for – could she be thinking of the *Sun*? – she hoped that her audience would not produce 'the kind of thing you would not like to see on your living-room table or on the screen in your living-room'. If the communicators were unable to achieve the self-discipline and self-regulation necessary to prevent such excesses, then 'we, as a matter of public policy . . . must simply protect our young people from some of the violence and pornography'. In spite of her desire to constrain the powers of Government and to increase the powers of the people, she would make every effort to achieve this end.

It looked very much as if the White Paper, when it eventually appeared, would reflect this mix of free marketeering and regulation. The worry was that while Mrs Thatcher's expressed concerns were with violence and pornography (how much pornography has there ever been on television except under the exceedingly free market systems like that in Italy?), what was believed to have fuelled her disapproval of television was the way in which the BBC handled terrorism in Northern Ireland. In the political atmosphere of triumphant Thatcherism other offending material might be seen off our screens than the odd nipple – awkward minority views, access programmes such as producers working both in the BBC and for Channel 4 had contrived to foster and with some difficulty keep alive.

When the White Paper at last appeared, complete with a coloured centrefold which must have pushed up the production costs considerably, it became apparent that it was inspired by the ideology of the market.

Broadcasting in the '90's

The title of the White Paper was already an indication of the line it would follow: *Broadcasting in the '90's: Competition, Choice and Quality*. The very title contained a reversal of priorities, for traditionally the aims had been quality and choice; competition (if accepted, as it had been) was a means to these aims. In fact one needed to read no further to know that the market forces were to be seen as the determinants of broadcasting policy. In line with the Thatcher Government's statements when introducing such steps as various privatisation measures and the poll tax, the proclaimed purpose of the specific proposals laid out in the White Paper is the extension of the citizen's liberties. The Government, says the first sentence, 'places the viewer at the centre of broadcasting policy'. It intends to open the doors so that individuals can choose for themselves from a wider range of programmes and types of broadcasting without detriment to programme standards and quality. The viewer will have not only a greater choice but 'a greater say'; but presumably not through greater access, through consultative processes, advisory committees, representation on governing bodies of broadcasting institutions, but through the consumer's power to buy or not buy the goods on offer.

The White Paper is anxious to remove anxieties about the possible contradictions between the desire to increase competition and the expressed desire to maintain standards. 'Both are essential if the quality of British broadcasting is to be safeguarded and enhanced into the next century.' It might have added that the two are not always easily reconcilable.

A careful reading of the document reveals signs of the tug between the two aims. In this respect the text is like a medieval manuscript in which scholars can detect the work of two scribes, each with his own attitude to the work in hand. In the case of the White Paper it is possible to detect in much the same way the work of two hands, one belonging presumably to the Home Office (worried about taste and decency and standards) and the other to the Department of Trade and Industry (determined to let slip the dogs of the market).

The blueprint for the future

The salient points in the White Paper can be summarised as follows:

1. the BBC to continue as 'the cornerstone of British broadcasting' but the licence fee to be eventually replaced by subscription;
2. the IBA (and the Cable Authority) to be replaced by the Independent Television Commission (ITC) operating with 'a lighter touch' but 'tough sanctions'. It will also be responsible for DBS;
3. the ITV network to be replaced by a regionally based Channel 3 freer to respond to market conditions;
4. a new national channel (with a less than universal signal) – Channel 5 – to be set up with the possibility of Channel 6 in the future;
5. Channel 4 to continue with its remit to be innovative but to be self-funded, i.e. competing for advertising with Channel 3 with the possibility of a financial safety-net;
6. a new Radio Authority with a 'light touch' to oversee an extended commercial radio system with five new national services;
7. all television services (including those of the BBC) to be free to raise money by subscription and sponsorship. All (except the BBC) to be free to carry advertising;
8. the Broadcasting Standards Council to safeguard standards on taste and decency and the portrayal of sex and violence;
9. the role of independent producers in programme-making to grow;
10. where ownership in the independent sector is concerned, controls on takeovers will be removed but the need for 'limits of ownership and on excessive cross-media ownership' is recognised but no hard proposals are made.

The cornerstone of British broadcasting

The section of the White Paper dealing with the BBC is rather short. It reiterates the BBC's duty to provide high-quality programming across the full range of tastes and interests and to offer the three ingredients of public service broadcasting: education, information and cultural material, and entertainment. The Corporation is also encouraged to pursue efficiency. This rather summary discussion of 'the cornerstone of British broadcasting' is no doubt explained by the fact that the future role and constitution of the Corporation will be fully discussed before the BBC's Charter comes up for renewal in 1996.

The White Paper is chiefly concerned with the BBC's method of financing its operations. One of Peacock's criticisms of the BBC, as we have seen, was that there was no direct cash nexus between the members of the audience and the Corporation, which was felt to be deleterious to the interests of both parties. (Not that there had been any noticeable outcry by the general public at this state of affairs.) It is logical therefore that the crucial paragraph in the White Paper dealing with the BBC should be headed 'The licence fee and subscription' or that it should contain proposals which, if they pass into law, must radically alter the nature of the BBC as a public service organisation.

> As new television services proliferate, the system of financing the BBC television and radio services by a compulsory licence fee alone will become harder to sustain. Though the Government accepts . . . that a sudden, wholesale switch to subscription would be undesirable and damaging, there should be a greater role for subscription. The Government looks forward to the eventual replacement of the licence fee . . .

To enable the BBC to fulfil these desires on the part of Government it will be authorised to encrypt its services so that, when subscription comes in, viewers will be unable to receive the service without payment and the use of a decoder. The extent and pace of the move to subscription will be for the BBC to judge, but, the Paper reiterates, 'the BBC will have in mind the objective of replacing the licence fee'. In the meantime 'to provide a financial incentive' the Government will, from 1991 on, decrease the licence fee in a way that reflects the BBC's success in generating income from subscription: in other words the more money from subscription, the less from the licence fee. The introduction of subscription will, the Paper adds, have the beneficial effect of ending 'the insulation of the BBC from its customers and from market disciplines'. In the same free enterprise spirit the BBC will be allowed to use the night hours on one of its channels for specialised subscription services. (It already runs one for doctors.)

The aim is very clear. In due course the licence fee will go and the BBC will depend on subscription and sponsorship to finance its television services. What the implications are for the BBC's radio services is not spelt out – 'account will need to be taken in due course of the implications for financing [them]'; which might be cynically interpreted as meaning that the Government has not thought about them or else that the solution is not easy. But the results of the measures are inevitably that the BBC will no longer offer a universal 'free' signal.

Significantly there is no discussion in the White Paper of how under the new dispensation the BBC will be able to continue to function as a cultural institution and patron of the arts, especially music.

Another monopoly broken

The burden of Peacock's criticisms had been aimed at the 'cosy duopoly' and the ITV monopoly of the advertising market for television. There was also a feeling among the proponents of the free market that the IBA was too meddlesome, too strict on the one hand in discharging its deregulatory duties and too liberal on the other in what it was prepared to allow on the screen. It is natural therefore that it is when dealing with the IBA and ITV, the commercial network it controls, that the White Paper is most explicit and introduces the most detailed changes. First and foremost the IBA is to be replaced as the regulatory body for all television services (of which, as we have seen, more than one is planned) by an Independent Television Commission (ITC) which will 'apply lighter, more objective programme require-ments'. (What is meant by 'objective' is not spelt out.) It will also be expected to act as a licensing body rather than a broadcasting authority and will be responsible for awarding franchises and defining the franchise areas. It will also license satellite programmes uplinked from the UK and provide 'consumer protection oversight' of these services. The regu-latory functions of the ITC are therefore to be vestigial. The question, then, is who is going to enforce those standards of decency to which Mrs Thatcher referred in her speech to the Press Association – who will control the portrayal of sex and violence? Not market forces because as any corner-shop distri-buting video cassettes shows there is a thriving market for softish porn and violence. Somebody must be responsible for what in an inelegant formulation the White Paper calls the 'consumer protection aspects of programme standards'.

Consumer protection

The answer is a new body – the Broadcasting Standards Council – which has already been set up and will in due course be placed on a statutory footing. It is required because the Government recognises 'the unique power of the broadcasting media to shape perceptions and their influence over attitudes and actions'. The power of radio and television, it warns, must not be abused.

The Council is already busy drawing up codes on the portrayal of sex and violence and standards of taste and decency (but did these not already exist, having been elaborated by the IBA?). It is also expected to monitor standards in TV and radio programmes received in the UK (i.e. by satellite) and in video works (but do the latter not already come under the Board of Film Classification, formerly the British Board of Film Censors?); and to undertake research on the effects of the portrayal of violence etc. in the media (but is there not already a plethora of academic work on this topic which, in the main, appears to demonstrate that the effect of television on behaviour and in particular its part – if any – in encouraging violence is difficult to prove?). All this monitoring is to be funded by a ridiculously low budget of £80,000 per annum.

The White Paper leaves open the eventual relationship between the Standards Council and the Broadcasting Complaints Commission. Their functions are clearly different – one dealing with codes and questions of taste and the other with specific complaints from viewers or listeners about unfair treatment and invasions of privacy. It seems to be a situation which will give rise to demarcation problems between the two organisations as each defends its own territory and interests. The Government will make up its mind 'in the light of experience'. It is difficult to see the reason for this hesitancy in a Government ready to be bloody, bold and resolute in other fields of broadcasting.

The advertising lobby

It is fundamental to the Government's case for change that it must respond to the 'growing concern on the part of the advertisers at the cost of television advertising and at the absence of effective competition in the sale of air time'. Here is how one advertising executive – Paul Bainsfair, Managing Director of Saatchi & Saatchi – described the situation. No doubt this was the kind of case presented to the Government:

> There are a number of contractors, based on a regional
> level, that provide the independent service to the
> viewers. Take for example Yorkshire. There is a
> company which has got the right to advertise
> independently in that area and they can sell time to

advertising agencies, and they also sell the time for Channel 4. This means that they could charge really whatever the market would bear but they weren't competing – as they would be in America – with another network and therefore the natural forces of market competition aren't in play. And actually it is worse than that because they operate local rates for local advertisers so that they can artificially shorten the availability of air time by selling a large amount of local air time, which would force the big advertisers to fight even harder among themselves for less time, driving up the price.

The advertising industry is an important and effective lobby which played a crucial part in the birth of ITV in the Fifties; its methods appear to have been less flamboyant in the period when the Thatcher Government was shaping its thoughts on the future of broadcasting. But play a part in shaping them it undoubtedly did by lobbying politicians and civil servants, as the Director General of the Institute of Practitioners in Advertising makes clear.

We had been lobbying on the subject of the problem of the commercial television monopoly for some years. When we began this in the early Eighties I think the politicians did not understand the way that television worked. They did not understand the extent to which the industry was unhappy with the structure of commercial television and the monopoly. And they certainly did not understand the government's determination to bring in free markets in every kind of business. In addition politicians and civil servants did not understand that there were opportunities to have additional channels . . . Then about two years ago the government realised that they had to adapt to the structure of the Nineties – they had to find a structure which would fit the market of the Nineties.

A new structure

The new structure is based in part on the fact that two new channels for television have suddenly become available. Many people had long felt that there must be room on the spectrum for more channels, but interested parties – such as BBC engineers, the military and other services – had always resisted the suggestion. Now there will be three and possibly four commercial channels: Channel 3 (the old ITV), Channel 4, Channel 5 and (a remote possibility) Channel 6.

Channels 5 and 6

The White Paper proposes that Channel 5 should come on stream from the beginning of 1993. It will be free to choose a mix of advertising and subscription for its revenue, thus bringing what is described as 'significant relief to the advertising market', which, being interpreted, means breaking the ITV monopoly on advertising.

Although defined as 'national in scope' Channel 5 will not be able to have national coverage. Reception problems such as interference from stations across the Channel are likely to limit its reach to 70 per cent with conditions particularly bad in the South-East, which is, for once, to lose out.

The Government envisages the Channel as possibly being divided up between various operators, each having a time segment to fill. For reasons that are unclear but which are presumably the same as apply to the privatised electricity industry, the Government believes that this will promote competition (between the operators? between channels?) and also enhance diversity.

When Channel 6 will come on stream (if it ever does) will depend on the development of microwave facilities which are still the subject of feasibility studies. The channel might provide a local service or be used for some form of subscription like Pay-as-you-view.

Channel 3

Channel 3, the one at present occupied by ITV, will be occupied by a regionally based operation replacing the present ITV set-up. The exact boundaries of franchise areas will be drawn under the new ITC and will not necessarily be the same as they are at present. Although the Channel 3 station will be required to show regional programming, it is probable that this redrawing of boundaries will eliminate some of the smaller ITV companies.

There will no longer be a network overseen by a regulatory authority and based on a system of cross-subsidies, although the companies may come to arrangements among themselves. More importantly, the ITC will no longer be 'the broadcaster'. The broadcasters will be the individual companies.

But the most fundamental changes concern the allocation of the franchises. Here the Government's intention is to introduce a 'more commercial element' into the allocation of franchises. This is envisaged as a two-stage process.

In the first of these the applicants will have to pass 'a quality threshold' which is not precisely defined. Opportunities for greater choice (with the prospect of ten or more channels in the future) mean, says the White Paper, that there is 'no longer the same need for quality of service to be prescribed by legislation or regulatory fiat'. Balance, that other slogan of public service, will be 'sorted out' by the viewers themselves as they move from channel to channel. Channel 3 will therefore have 'positive programme obligations' but also 'greater freedom to match its programming to market conditions'. These requirements are so vague that it does not look as if many applicants will fail to clear the first hurdle.

The second stage in the process is another matter. Here (unless, as seems probable, the proposals are modified) the market will reign; for 'the ITC would be required to select the applicant . . . who had submitted the highest tender'. As a sop – a gesture towards public accountability – the procedures will be open to public scrutiny at both stages. (How? by whom? Will the opening of the sealed tenders be any different from a lottery draw?) The consequences of making franchises over to the applicants with the deepest pockets will fundamentally alter the system and might well restrict the field to a handful of financial magnates who are already declaring their intention of bidding. Tendering, the White Paper believes, would be a 'more objective' way of giving access to a public resource; which it certainly is in the limited sense that £x million is, objectively speaking, more than £x − y million. Another way of putting it is that the Government believes that the ability to sign a cheque is more important than the ability to formulate a programme policy. Unless the system is altered – and there are signs that the Government is having second thoughts in the face of criticisms of the proposal – cash will be a substitute for value judgements.

Channel 4

That leaves Channel 4, which the White Paper acknowledges has been 'a striking success'. Its remit is envisaged as continuing as at present – to provide innovation, range, diversity and quality – but changes in its funding are believed to be necessary. There is a strong case, the Paper argues, for funding the channel from its own advertising, which would lead to greater competition between the commercial television channels: a demand that has been pressed by the advertisers who have 'paid for the independent television system' (as have, it might be added, the audience in that each purchase they make has an element in its price that funds the advertising in the first place). Here, once again, the advertising lobby has a victory to chalk up.

At present Channel 4 depends on a subscription from the ITV companies in the sum of about £181.5 million per annum. The Government, which does not believe in subsidies, would like all financial and structural links with Channel 3 to be broken off. Channel 4 would then be an independent organisation subject to the light touch regulation of the ITC. How precisely it should be organised is left open but several options are discussed in the White Paper.

1. it could be a private company licensed (after competitive tender) by the ITC which (exceptionally) would have to enforce the licence conditions 'rigorously'. It could fund itself by selling air time, by subscription or by sponsorship;
2. it could be a non-profit-making subsidiary of the ITC free to use advertising, subscription or sponsorship but with a guaranteed minimum level of income which could be a percentage of the advertising revenue of the independent television system; or
3. there could be some sort of link – a kind of complementarity – between Channels 4 and 5, which would allow them to compete with the other channels.

The White Paper leaves the options open. The decision will be a political one.

The independents again

Channel 4 set a new pattern in having no in-house productions. Instead it relies on independent producers, a term which extends from companies with considerable production resources to small production units. The Government is anxious, for its own ideological and political reasons, to extend the practice. It has already set the BBC and ITV a target of 25 per cent of original material from independent producers by 1992. After 1992 the proposal in the White Paper is that in the commercial television sector 'no licensee should be required by the ITC to maintain any in-house production capacity'.

Direct broadcasting by satellite

The IBA is responsible for DBS, and the ITC will take over that duty later, exercising 'consumer protection oversight' and enforcing any international obligations accepted by the Government under agreements with other European countries on standards and advertising practices. So far it has only one DBS contractor: British Satellite Broadcasting (BSB), whose investors include Anglia Television, Granada Television, Reed International (the powerful publishing group), Pearsons, and Next, the retail dress shop chain. The largest single holding is that of Bond, the Australian media magnate, whose financial empire has been going through considerable difficulties. BSB, which owns its own satellite, has been favoured by Government. It has been granted a fifteen-year contract, the length of which reflects doubts about the profitability of the operation and in particular about the success of subscription; its main attraction – the Movie Channel with a catalogue of 1,800 films – will be encrypted from 6 p.m. through the night and will cost something like £10 a month.

> The original concept [says Bob Hunter of BSB] that won the franchise for BSB is still intact and that is finding a new way to fund television and expanding the ways in which television is funded. That is by having a subscription channel and the main locomotive drive is the movie channel which is high quality American and British movies that people will pay money for to see on television at a point well before they normally appear on free television. That is the basic premiss. What drove the application in 1986 is that the government and everyone is talking about subscription television. That subscription movie channel was always backed up by the idea of a live channel with news, events, sport – that was the Now Channel – and another channel which was general entertainment. What we have done is to refine these concepts with the prospect in the White Paper of a five channel DBS system coming on-stream.

The other programmes offered by BSB will be advertising-supported; they are a news and sports channel and a daytime channel – produced by Yorkshire Television and the *Daily*

Mail, aimed at 'women at home, younger adults and children'. The aim is to counter-balance the older down-market bias of the ITV audience. The promotion literature spoke of 'greater viewer choice and more quality programming'. The aim of BSB is to emerge as 'the third force in British broadcasting' by providing a national service, for it does not believe 'that for the foreseeable future there will be a real pan-European television market'. Meanwhile it will concentrate on competing against what it sees as a 'largely fragmented terrestrial competitor'. BSB expects to reach around 4 million homes by 1993 and 8 million by 1997. It proposes to transmit using a signal which has a higher capacity – that is, can transmit more information – than the present PAL system used in our sets. The extra capacity will make it possible to transmit and receive a better picture and digital sound. This is seen as being the first step towards High Definition Television (HDTV), which will give a larger and even better picture.

Over twenty satellite channels using mostly low-power satellites can be received in Britain, given the requisite receiving equipment – a receiving dish of more than a metre in diameter – although the British public is not their prime target. One channel specifically aimed at this country, the Lifestyle Channel, has been in operation since 1985. It belongs to a group consisting of British Telecom, W. H. Smith and Maxwell of the Mirror Group. Lifestyle is described as 'every woman's friend' and is largely dependent on American soap operas supplemented by keep-fit and cookery programmes and romance. The handouts claim that within a year of its inception it was 'firmly established' in the United Kingdom; but no figures are given for homes capable of receiving the signal. The only figure is for Eire where they claim that a quarter of a million viewers enjoy 'the delights of the channel'.

Then there is Astra, a medium-power sixteen-channel satellite launched in 1988 carrying eleven English-language channels and five channels for other European countries. Based in Luxembourg, Astra is owned by a group of European investors who include Thames Television. (Once again – as in the case of BSB – an ITV contractor is diversifying and covering itself against developments in what may be an uncertain future.) Rupert Murdoch of News International, who already has interests in the European satellite business, has leased six channels on Astra and – eager to get in ahead of BSB – has launched a satellite service – Sky Television. He has been accused of blatantly using his five UK newspapers ranging from *The Times* to the *Sun* to mount a campaign boosting his venture and denigrating the BBC and the licence fee.

The services on offer are Sky Channel, a twenty-four-hour entertainment programme with the best games shows and 'the most addictive soap operas from around the world' broadcast in blocks of five daily. It also gives viewers 'another chance' (that means repeats of old material) to see 'thrilling action series' along with 'perennial favourites' like *The Lucy Show*; Sky News promises a comprehensive news service and programmes like *Target* with Norman Tebbit and Austin Mitchell; Eurosport is 'the all-sport, all-action channel'; Sky Movies has important agreements with big Hollywood studios like Warner Brothers and Twentieth Century Fox. Having started as a free programme it will be encrypted to become 'a premium pay-TV channel'. Sky also planned to offer the Disney channel (also encrypted) as 'magical entertainment for everyone in the family' and Sky Arts providing 'hours and hours of quality entertainment' from 'Elgar to Ellington, Hogarth to Hockney, Pinter to Pasternak'. But Disney has withdrawn amid threats of billion-dollar lawsuits and the Arts Channel has been replaced by another 'classic film' channel, which usually means old B movies.

These programmes are transmitted using the current PAL system. They require a different dish from that used by BSB. Planning permission will be required to have two dishes. None of these channels comes under the IBA. Because it is distributed largely by cable – at the time of writing only about 50,000 homes can get the signal directly by dish – Sky Television is overseen by the Cable Authority. It is not clear from the White Paper what exact powers the ITC will have over satellite channels which are not uplinked from the UK but are distributed here by cable systems. No doubt with fears in mind of porn and violence being beamed in by satellite, the White Paper gives assurances that the programme content of all such services will be supervised. What is also unclear is the degree to which the ITC will be able to intervene over such matters as the accuracy of news services, the balance of news and current affairs programmes.

The limits of free enterprise

The White Paper expresses the determination to keep ownership in the independent sector widely spread. The controls on take-overs are to be removed; this means that financial interests which have not passed the 'quality' test could take over a franchise. The Government is, however, conscious that there are dangers in the concentration of ownership and in excessive cross-media ownership. The kinds of ownership it no doubt had in mind were Rupert Murdoch's string of five papers in the United Kingdom and his stake in Sky Television.

No sooner had the new arrangements for allocating the franchises been announced than Mr Maxwell, owner of the *Mirror*, who also has satellite interests, let it be known that he was interested in acquiring Central Television's Midland franchise in which he has a 19.8 per cent holding; whereupon the Office of Fair Trading expressed some alarm. Mr Murdoch, for his part, launched Sky channel in the spring of 1989 using his newspapers – which together account for 35 per cent of the circulation of the British press – to boost the new channel and to mount a campaign against the BBC and the licence fee. Such cross-ownership alarmed the Tory chairman of the Home Affairs Select Committee, who said in the House that it was wrong in principle and could lead to a distortion of free competition. Journalists, he said, could be forced to write favourably about their proprietors' television interests.

It was no doubt because of such concerns that the Home Secretary announced strict limits to newspaper ownership in commercial television.

No national newspaper owner will be allowed to own more than 20 per cent of any commercial television franchise, direct broadcasting by satellite channel or national radio franchise. The Government also stated that there was a strong case for debarring national newspaper owners from having a significant financial interest in more than one franchise. These rules will thwart Mr Maxwell's ambitions, but they will not prevent Mr Murdoch from taking large stakes in other European satellites like Astra, which uses a non-UK frequency and is therefore not subject to the Independent Broadcasting Authority. He will not, however, be able to hold more than 20 per cent of any commercial television franchise. This still leaves a gap which the chairman of the Home Affairs Select Committee suggested should be closed by ordering users of satellites like Astra to divest their UK newspaper interests.

Cable

The White Paper is rather summary in its treatment of cable and has to admit that 'the growth of new cable systems has been slow'. (One reason is the hesitation on the part of financial interests to put money into a system with high capital costs and no likelihood of a quick return on investment.) Jon Davey, the Director of the Cable Authority – which, under legislation passed in 1984, is responsible for franchising cable and for regulating the content of the services provided – identifies the problem as a cultural barrier, which he believes is coming down fast. He comforts himself with the thought that the British public has always been slow to take up new media developments. 'They were slow to take up television, a little faster to take up colour television, and the video recorder. If you look at the pattern of take-up on all these things it starts off slowly in the early years and then the curve climbs rapidly.'

There has been a good deal of lobbying by the cable operators for the Cable Authority – which already has indirect control over low-power satellite channels in that it distributes their signal – to also have control of all satellite television, including DBS. But the Home Office has always regarded DBS as 'broadcasting' and has therefore rejected the suggestion. Consequently the White Paper proposes that the ITC will assume the powers and duties of the Cable Authority, as George Russell, the Chairman of the IBA, explains.

> Cable will come under the ITC and the Cable Authority will, as far as I'm concerned, just move in and probably become a small sub-division of the ITC which specialises in cable because it is very different from dealing with terrestrial television. So you are likely to have two or three strands within the ITC of which cable is one.

Radio

National commercial services

When it comes to radio the White Paper believes, in line with the Government's general philosophy, that it is 'feasible and healthy' to face the BBC with competition. There will therefore be 'at least three' national commercial services competing with the BBC.

These services will not operate within the framework of public service broadcasting. That is to say, there will be no requirement to inform, educate and entertain (though they may 'follow a public service pattern if they wish'). They will, however, be expected to provide a diverse programme service respecting the norms of taste and decency but not giving 'undue prominence to views on religious matters or matters of political or industrial controversy'; which is a new formulation of the rules on controversy – or rather one that harks back to the bad old days before the war when controversy was actively discouraged.

The franchises for the new stations will be allocated by competitive tender. These new stations will come under a new 'slim' Radio Authority – the use of the language of fashion copywriting is interesting – supervising them with a lighter touch and more 'flexibly' where advertising and sponsorship are concerned.

Local radio?

On local radio the White Paper is vague, talking of creating 'an environment in which community radio . . . will be able to fulfil its potential'. In 1986 the Government announced that there would be an experiment in community radio, but, as a Home Office consultative document says in a dead-pan way, 'in the event the experiment did not take place'. The reason is interesting and significant. It was because 'it proved difficult to construct a regulatory framework . . . within existing legislation' that would not have involved Government in control of what went on the air. What this means is that the voices that wish to be heard and the groups that would apply for licences to broadcast are not necessarily ones the Government wishes to encourage – voices from the ethnic minorities and from the inner cities, for instance. A government which has consistently centralised power and reduced local intervention in local politics must find it difficult to give access to local voices, particularly in a system that exercises a lighter touch.

BBC radio

The White Paper passes over the future of BBC radio lightly by saying that the BBC's radio services 'will continue to be funded by the licence fee for some years to come. But BBC radio services will be subject to a much stronger stimulus of competition.' But the future of the licence fee is in doubt and

BBC Television may well find itself competing with the commercial channels on a reduced budget. Where, then, is BBC radio to draw its funds from? If there are cuts, how will it be able to continue to provide its present programme policy, which ranges over pop, classical and modern music, poetry and the arts?

The White Paper is a radical document.

That there had to be change was inevitable. Technological advances saw to that. But it is nowhere said that the mechanisms of the market had to be used so relentlessly. What some people find distressing in a document that deals with media which are socially and culturally of immense importance is that although lip service is paid to social and cultural values, the discourse employed by the Paper is overwhelmingly that of consumerism and of commercial profit. Looking to the future and trans-national broadcasting, the Paper sees in it the possibility of television playing 'a unique role in international trade'. The criticism which is being increasingly levelled at the Thatcher Government – that it has no cultural policy – is given added weight by this document.

PART TWO

The White Paper – Debate and Reactions

The first part of this book was a historical review of how attitudes towards the nature, organisation and aims of British broadcasting, which has, since its inception, worked within the framework of public service, have changed. That review ended with the White Paper published in November 1988, which proposes radical changes in both television and radio.

In the second part the issues raised by the White Paper and the effects it will have, if it becomes law, on the shape and nature of British broadcasting are discussed by broadcasters, advertisers and trade unionists. The interviews were carried out by Garret O'Leary.

ELEVEN

'Structured Turbulence'

The changes which have overtaken British broadcasting in the past, such as the arrival of commercial television in the Fifties, aroused controversy. Yet, looked at from today's historical perspective, that break in the solid monopolistic tradition was less far-reaching than what the 1988 White Paper proposes. Those who are professionally involved in the media, as broadcasters, journalists, academics or advertisers, are sometimes accused of being obsessed with issues like those raised in the White Paper. Are the general public equally interested? Is not television, or radio, for them something that is simply there like water, taken for granted and in some sense 'free'? Indeed, how much do the general public, or even – to use a narrower definition – how much do teachers, lecturers, professional people and 'the chattering classes' in general know about how broadcasting is organised? The answer is usually very little. It follows that they may not yet fully realise the nature and scope of the changes proposed. The Home Office invited responses to the White Paper and received some 3,000 of them – some from organisations like trade unions, parents' associations, or university departments, some from individuals or from MPs writing on behalf of constituents. The Home Office declares itself well pleased with the response. But it is still a tiny figure compared to the almost 19 million licence-holders. It must be doubted whether the television audience are fully aware of the choices that will face them over the next decade.

The cornerstone of public service broadcasting

When considering the future of British broadcasting as it is foreshadowed in the White Paper it is easiest to start with the BBC, which is at first glance not deeply – or at least not immediately – affected. It is recognised to have 'a special role' and will remain 'in the foreseeable future' (which means in effect until 1996 when the Charter comes up for renewal) 'the cornerstone of British broadcasting' although it is warned that it must not 'insulate itself against change'. The BBC's reaction has therefore been one of calm satisfaction, which is politically wise whatever misgivings there may be under the surface about the final fate of the Corporation, which, as a previous Director General remarked, is not necessarily eternal. The present Director General, however, is not unhappy.

> I think we have had assurances in the White Paper. We
> are asked to be the cornerstone of British broadcasting.
> That is a good assurance in a White Paper which
> emerged after two years of discussions at the highest
> levels of government . . . We will move into Charter
> renewal on 1st January 1997 and we will hope very much
> then that our cornerstone role will be confirmed . . .

This feeling of security is echoed by Sir Ian Trethowan, an ex-Director General of the BBC who is now Chairman of Thames Television.

> I think it [the White Paper] will make the BBC more
> secure. It will obviously unsettle the present inhabitants
> of commercial television to a degree because they're
> going to have to think very carefully about the sort of
> investments they make and how they are going to
> operate . . . I think the BBC should emerge from it as
> very strong and the cornerstone of broadcasting in this
> country – and one would hope of the production of high
> quality programming. They say in the White Paper that

that is their intention . . . I trust they will keep to that
intention and make sure that it [the BBC] is able to do it and
is properly fuelled to do it. I hope they will forget the idea
of subscription on the BBC.

It is the view, too, of the Chairman and Managing Director of
London Weekend Television, Brian Tesler.

The BBC will become as they were before ITV ever
began – the dominant broadcaster in this country
because its revenue is assured by the licence fee – change
won't even be contemplated until 1996 when the
possibilities of subscription will be canvassed . . . So on
the one hand you will have all the rest – Channel 3,
Channel 4, Channel 5, night-time franchises and all the
satellite channels. This will make the BBC far and away
the dominant broadcaster in this country, which is
something one hesitates to believe was intended by the
Conservative Government. What they have done is to
secure its strength.

Melvyn Bragg of LWT agrees.

They're very hard to fight – the BBC. ITV has fought for
years and it still has to fight every week just to slightly
edge ahead of them. They've got a totally subsidised
system and are richer than us in many ways . . . The
BBC moans about money. It is one of the richest
broadcasting organisations in resources and money in the
world. They can always outbid ITV and they often do.
They can outbid them for stars; they can outbid them for
properties; they can outbid them in the time they spend
on things. And good luck to them. It just means that if a
cheap ITV system is against them they will wipe the
floor with it.

That, of course, presumes that the BBC is going to be able to
maintain its present level of funding, which is not necessarily
the case. Not everyone is so sanguine about the BBC's future or
about the degree to which the title of 'the cornerstone of British
broadcasting' is some sort of guarantee for the future. Certainly

Tony Hearn, the Secretary General of BETA (Broadcasting and Entertainment Trades Alliance), one of the two unions concerned with broadcasting, is not optimistic and holds that the future of public service broadcasting is very grim unless the present government is turned out of office.

> I don't think the Government regards the BBC as the cornerstone of public service broadcasting although that phrase appears in the White Paper. As *we* see the White Paper they want the BBC to go from the licence fee to subscription. Ten years from now, say, the BBC in its present form can't survive on subscription.

This is a view shared by Alan Sapper, the General Secretary of ACTT, the other communications union, who finds the future of public service broadcasting 'very grim indeed'. The BBC will represent the last residual of public service broadcasting – but not for long.

> They're not secure at all because if they perform a public service broadcasting role it will mean that their news and information services will cross-examine the Government – and one thing the Government can't stand is a cross-examination of their policies and their actions – and then they will act against the BBC as they've acted against ITV. Now they are acting against it in a predictable way. They're saying You should go on to subscription television – your income should not come from the licence fee but from subscription television.

This, naturally enough, is not a view shared by the Director General of the BBC.

> I don't think the BBC concept of public service is under threat . . . We've clearly been putting our money where our mouth is. We've been putting money into strengthening our news and current affairs which I think is a core activity of a public service broadcaster . . . We're putting money into arts programming; we've

strengthened some of our schools broadcasting by confirming involvement in the national curriculum . . . I think we are clear that we are the cornerstone of public service broadcasting – that's what our role is. So we're not under threat in that sense so long as we have enough money to fulfil the role.

Will the BBC continue to have enough money to fulfil its public service role? That is the crucial question.

There is certainly a reading of the White Paper which can lead one to think that the BBC will be expected to be increasingly dependent (and that before 1996) on subscription. It is worthwhile recalling the precise terms used in the White Paper.

> The Government looks forward to the eventual replacement of the licence fee . . . The Government accordingly proposes to authorise the BBC to encrypt its services so that it can raise money through subscription . . . the BBC will have in mind the objective of replacing the licence fee.

The Government's intention seems to be stated with considerable clarity in this passage. Taking it at its face value, one is bound to consider two difficult questions which the BBC's spokesmen (for it is not only the Director General who takes this line) are apparently not anxious to broach at present.

One refers to the BBC's ability to cover its costs by subscription.

In the year 1986/87, the BBC's gross income from the licence was over £1,020 million, which was supplemented by trading profits from the sale of programmes and various kinds of merchandising. After deductions for tax and the fee to the Post Office for collecting the revenue, the BBC was left with just under £1,000 million. A year's television costs around £655 million to produce and radio some £240 million. Can subscription provide an income of this magnitude to support the present scale of production in television? How does radio get funded?

And what happens to the patronage which the BBC provides, for instance, to orchestras?

The second is a corollary to the first. If it cannot raise funds of that order, what becomes of the BBC as a public service organisation providing a broad mix of programmes?

But apart from these very difficult financial questions, subscription presents considerable problems of another kind. The advocates of subscription argue that by going over to that method of funding, wholly or in part, the BBC would be better able to meet the needs of the viewer (or consumer, as they prefer to say). How is this to be achieved except in a negative way – in the sense that if few people watch a programme it may (in certain circumstances) be considered a failure and not to have matched up to the audience's desires? But it is not at all easy to discover what the viewers really want or what the unsatisfied desires are of which the free marketeers so confidently talk. Janet Street-Porter, who has worked as a producer in ITV and is now with the BBC, puts her finger on the problem.

> I would say from my own experience that some form of subscription to replace the licence fee is a somewhat Utopian dream and that if we want subscription television it is a very different kind of television to what the BBC provide. Because, as everybody knows full well, if you ask the consumer: What do you want? What are you prepared to pay for? they say the obvious – they say, drama, comedy, this that and the other. They don't tend to choose the small things that give them great pleasure but which they haven't yet seen. It's the same in audience research, we never ask people What kind of programme do you want? We ask them about things that pleased them, or to which they responded or they remember and from that we deduce the kind of programming we should be making more of. If you say to subscribers What do you want to pay for? they'll say they'll pay more for the mainstream and not for what I think makes the BBC unique – which is all the other kinds of programming it puts out . . . I think the BBC is

unique because it spends a great deal of time and money trying to create a mix of programming that hopefully reflects the diversity of the population in a way that hardly any other channels in the world do . . . I think that if subscription was brought in it would just create a very bland diet, to be perfectly honest.

Concerns about the effects of subscription are shared by Mark Shivas, Head of Drama Group, BBC Television.

The requirement that we drift towards subscription – I don't think anyone has thought it out properly. My gut reaction is that British television is widely regarded around the world as the least worst television there is. It seems perverse to me to try to break up the things that are working well at the moment – particularly the BBC.

And here is another voice, that of Bill Cotton, formerly Managing Director of BBC Television:

Subscription is no answer for the BBC. Subscription is an elitist type of programming and the BBC has never been an elitist organisation. So I hope they will forget the idea of a subscription on the BBC.

But if the BBC were not to have recourse to subscription how else might they raise funds? The sums in question, as we have seen, are large. The cost of providing programmes (excluding regional programming) for the BBC's two national channels is over £600 million per annum. The Director General discusses the alternatives.

Advertising is ruled out in all ways. We want it ruled out. The Peacock Committee ruled it out. The Government White Paper rules it out. You are therefore left with three other methods of funding: one is a government grant, which certainly applies to our overseas broadcasting but would be inappropriate for domestic broadcasting. Secondly, there is the licence fee, and thirdly, there is subscription – and none of us knows how subscription is going to work. It is untried, it suits

premium services. It doesn't fit universality and public
service broadcasting.

To which, according to Bill Cotton, there seems to be only one
answer:

They should stay on the licence . . . People do not
consider the sort of value they get from the BBC for that
sort of money to be unacceptable. People generally don't
and that is across the board. Of course you find people
who don't want to pay it. I don't really want to pay
income tax. I know people who don't want to pay
anything – and I don't blame them. But if you are asking
me what is value for money – certainly to have a decently
civilised and properly organised broadcasting system as
far as the cultural life and the entertainment life of this
country is concerned – it is cheap at the price and most
people want it.

The official attitude of the BBC, however, as expressed by its
Director General when he was asked about the very specific
terms in which the White Paper talks about replacing the licence
fee, was relaxed.

We're all agreed, I think, that the licence is the method
of financing the BBC for the foreseeable future and I
think it is also clear from the various discussions we have
had and the announcements that have been made in
parliamentary debates and seminars that there will be a
review of funding of the BBC during the Charter renewal
process – but there won't be before then – so that
certainly up to 1997 the BBC will be firmly funded by
the licence fee. Then there will be a debate, as there
always is when we have a Charter renewal, about the
basis we move forward on now that the Labour Party has
asked for a similar review . . . But until that time the
licence fee will finance the BBC . . . We have argued in
our response to the White Paper that it is a cost effective
and appropriate method for funding universality of
public service broadcasting and we will no doubt be
arguing that in the mid-1990s as well.

Others like Bill Cotton, now outside the BBC, are more sceptical.

I think the BBC in one sense has come out of the White Paper very well in that it is defined as the cornerstone of British broadcasting. On the other hand, the BBC's continuing existence seems to me to be inadequately addressed. Great play is made with the licence – in my view the licence fee is very good value and frankly there is no serious discontent amongst the public about it – a number of newspapers whip up agitation about it from time to time but it's actually very good value for money and I think most people actually realise that. To think that the BBC could sustain the range of services it now does on television and on radio if it were to move to a larger subscription base – what is proposed in 1996 – I think is pie in the sky. And I think it would be a great loss to the public if that were to happen. So to that extent the BBC is in some danger in the longer term.

Might indeed the time not come when the BBC was not able to afford to make certain types of public service programmes? The Director General thinks not.

Not that I can see. No, I think we have always been inventive in keeping up the quality and range of our programming . . . Co-production is now a fundamental way of sharing production costs with other broadcasters and many BBC2 programmes wouldn't exist if it wasn't for co-production finance from outside. Previously BBC Enterprises didn't exist as an operation which put money into programmes. Since early this decade we've been putting substantial sums of money into BBC programmes through our commercial activities, and I think we've always been able to find ways of keeping up the quality and range of our programmes. I have every confidence that we will continue to do so. So I see no diminution in the range, nor do I see us withdrawing from areas of programme-making. It will be hard and we know that there is an inflationary pressure on the acquisition of programmes through films or whatever, competing with new entrants, and the cost of acquiring sporting rights will, I think, be extremely expensive . . . But I think that we will be sufficiently skilful managerially to actually find ways of raising funds to supplement our licence fee, which is indexed to the consumer price index. So I don't share the view that the BBC won't be able to afford quality drama or news and current affairs programmes. It simply doesn't stand up to scrutiny in my view. But it depends whether you are an optimist or a pessimist in this debate.

It may, of course, be that the BBC, which has a long and by no means guileless history of dealing with governments, is merely keeping its head down and saving its ammunition for battles in the run-up to the renewal of the Charter in the 1990s. So it may be a case of the BBC thinking, 'sufficient unto the day is the evil thereof'. Meanwhile in the view of David Nicholas, the Chief Executive of ITN, the real target of the Government's reformist zeal is ITV.

I think that in the cyclical way these things go, the heat is off the BBC for a while – although it remains to be seen just how serious [things are] when the Charter comes up and attention is turned to that. But I guess the ITV has really been the focus of the Government's attention in the White Paper and I think the BBC can take some comfort from being described as the cornerstone of British broadcasting.

The Other Public Service Monopoly

Since the decisions to be taken on the ultimate fate of the BBC
have been in effect postponed, the bulk of the recommendations
in the White Paper point to a radical restructuring of the ITV
network which has, in the words of the Chairman of the IBA,
brought about 'a major expansion in the public service broadcasting supplied by the commercial sector in the 1980s – for
example, Channel 4, extra daytime and night hours services'.
He goes on:

> This has been matched by a boom in advertising which
> has been in short supply, which has meant higher prices
> because of the demand of the industrial and commercial
> city business interests wanting advertising. That is a
> headlong rush in public service broadcasting . . . and it
> only needs that boom to turn down or advertising rates
> to drop and they're over-extended as an industry.
>   Secondly, competition which was barely thought of in
> mid-86, when Peacock finished, has started to pour in.
> Channel 5 hadn't been thought of. Channel 6 had never
> been considered. BSB was expected to have 3 channels,
> now there will be 5 DBS channels far sooner than
> expected. Sky wasn't talked about but now it seems
> Astra may offer 48 channels eventually. That's a lot of
> new competition chasing advertising revenue, which puts
> a major squeeze on public service broadcasting in the
> commercial sector. And the third thing that is important
> is that all the companies have become public companies,

quoted on the Stock Exchange, and now instead of just being producers trying to make a profit they've got to deliver higher share prices, higher dividends, and there's a pull away from money being used for programmes to money being used to match your proper City needs, whereas it used to just be matched to meet the interest bill. And it is a totally different management task and those three things are massively important.

The fourth is the ITV network itself . . . If you go through the figures you'll find that 8 to 10 per cent represents the total profitability of the ITV system. So you don't need too great a drop in either volume of advertising or price of advertising to lose the profitability of the system and to make public service broadcasting basically not affordable. That is the dilemma we are facing. The White Paper came along – and to me it is necessary to have a broadcasting bill because it is the catalyst that allows properly managed change to take place.

Much is indeed going to change, including the nature of the body charged with overseeing commercial broadcasting, which will include television, radio, cable and satellite transmissions. The diminution in its power is seen by some as controversial, as the IBA's Director of Television, David Glencross, makes clear.

In the 1990s the IBA will be replaced by a Commission which we hope will take on board very many features of the IBA – not excluding particularly the engineering ones, which are a major part of the IBA's staffing and expenditure both in terms of running the transmitters and engaging in basic engineering research, which we think is extremely valuable not just to the IBA and to television but to the country as a whole because a lot of the developments which our engineers (and for that matter the BBC's research engineers) have done have been taken up world-wide. It is a very important national asset.

The ITC will lose the degree of regulatory power which the IBA has had over 30 years. That means that the ITC will not be responsible for the schedules of ITV or Channel 4; they will not be the publisher of the programmes on ITV or Channel 4; they will not have any powers to amend programmes or indeed to stop programmes before transmission. That is naturally a controversial point. On the rare occasions when that sort of power has been exercised there have been great cries of censorship, inevitably. On these many more occasions when we've declined to intervene when we've been lobbied by various people to stop things happening, we've been accused of being toothless and impotent. All that debate will disappear – and maybe rightly, I think. With the proliferation of channels to have an Authority as publisher at one remove from the programme-making process I think probably doesn't make sense in the 1990s.

The White Paper acknowledges that 'the VHF networks run by the BBC and IBA give a highly effective service to the public' and that this 'considerable engineering achievement' is 'highly regarded internationally'. Nevertheless in pursuit of the same policies and the same profit motive as lie behind the privatisation of electricity and water it wishes to see a regionally based, privatised transmission system designed to promote competition. But has the problem of the transmission grid been thought out? David Glencross is dubious.

I think it has not been thought out at all in the White Paper. The idea that every region – however regions are defined – shall have its own privatised television transmission arrangements with sub-contractors seems to me to assume that privatising transmission arrangements is rather like privatising dustbins. It is very much more complicated than that. The whole system which we and the BBC have built up over the years is based on an extremely complicated and indeed an increasingly automated and centralised system of transmission.

The reaction of the ITV contractors

> 'We are in for three or four years of structured turbulence.'

That is the view of the Chairman of ITN. With that turbulence in the offing, how have the ITV contractors reacted to the White Paper? David Elstein, Director of Programmes at Thames Television, sees problems.

> The White Paper is something we must welcome as a document for discussion. It was obvious that, with the new technologies, maintaining the status quo of British broadcasting was not an option. Anything that does extend choice and quality should be welcomed. It's interesting to see that the White Paper does include repeated references to the Government's interest in maintaining choice and quality as well as encouraging competition; but it's how you achieve choice and quality which is my major concern, and in that respect I think the White Paper is very thin indeed on any evidence that persuades me that you can make compatible their free market approach to broadcasting with their ambition to maintain the present standards and provide a genuine extension of choice – not simply more of the same.

Brian Tesler, Chairman of LWT, also has his doubts about the possibility of programme standards being maintained.

> There's no question but that the range and diversity and quality generally of ITV programming is likely to suffer. It is likely to be eroded – bits are likely to fall off the ends and those bits are the ones that don't earn advertising revenue, that don't attract big audiences and therefore advertising revenue, because it is advertising revenue that pays for programmes. So it is quite possible that minority programming – by which I mean adult education and documentaries and children's programming and arts programming and local programming – will suffer.

Nor, paradoxically, in his view, will the changes proposed, which entail a proliferation of channels, necessarily produce the lower commercial rates the advertisers believe to have in their reach.

> The irony is that the new channels won't be able to afford popular quality drama and entertainment – it's expensive to make that kind of programme – and because ITV's own programming is likely to be impaired the result will be, ironically, that instead of the cost of air time reducing for the advertiser it will actually increase. Very simply – an advertiser buys impact. He buys the number of people reached by his advertisement. If he wants to reach x thousand people he can reach them with one commercial today in ITV. If ITV's audience is reduced and all the other channels have small audiences, in order to reach the same number of people he's going to have to buy perhaps five times as much air time. The accumulation of cost of all these spots – I'm simplifying – won't be less than the single spot was beforehand. And indeed the really valuable programmes that do attract big audiences are going to cost a hell of a lot more than they do now.

Another critical voice, that of Melvyn Bragg, concentrates on the proposal that the ITV contracts should be put up for auction and that the Independent Television Commission (ITC), the new regulatory body, should have a lighter touch than the present IBA.

> I think it [the White Paper] is a contradictory document – a confused document – and the more I talk to politicians the more I think it is a rather green White Paper and is susceptible to alteration. The thing is which areas will be altered. As it stands it is a blue print for the dismemberment of ITV.
> If they auction franchises and therefore make it almost by definition very expensive indeed to get a franchise – because people will bid up . . . if you make it expensive for people to get in, those who win the franchise will

obviously have to get their money back as fast as possible. Therefore their inclination is going to be toward shows which get their money back – and we all know what those shows are. They're down-market, mass appeal shows.

If at the same time you have a system where the regulation, i.e. the public service imposition, will be lightened and lessened, then you have a recipe for a service which does not cherish programmes like the *South Bank Show* like *World in Action* – which is probably the best weekly current affairs documentary slot there is in this country – such as high class drama and so forth.

There is also to be an increase in the levy, which is a fairly punitive tax on ITV anyway, leaving less money to make programmes. If you then tell the regulators that they needn't regulate much, then you have a recipe for down-market cheap television – inevitably. The logic goes further than that. It might become so expensive that the present broadcasters don't want to broadcast. London Weekend Television might decide it is too expensive to be a broadcaster – they'd rather be a publishing house. They own the copyright on all their own programmes so they will stop putting them on ITV and will sell them elsewhere – perhaps to satellite, perhaps to Channel 5, perhaps to the BBC, who knows?

He is not alone in his pessimism. David Elstein discusses the possibility that the ITV network will not survive as a system and that his company might not regain its franchise – in the sense that it could not afford to make a high enough bid for it. He is speaking against the background of new commercial relationships with independent producers and of competition from satellites.

What the White Paper adds to this is the prospect of quite a lot more competition – for instance with Channel 4 – and of a less integrated network – in other words one where there may be no network at all. It also holds out the prospect that – if we were successful in regaining our franchise – large chunks of our output would disappear

altogether: children's programmes, education programmes, religion, arts, most of our current affairs because
there would be no requirement to make them and therefore
no incentive to make them and therefore they would not get
made. I also think that the shape of our output, were we to
renew our franchise, would change. We would eliminate
quite a swathe of our drama output too and substitute
acquired programming for it.

It is, of course, possible that we won't regain our
franchise in which case this company would have to adjust
itself to being an independent producer within the UK and
a supplier of programmes to the international market-
place, which would eliminate our regional programming
too – unless we were able to sell regional programmes to the
incoming London weekday contractor – assuming that
there's a weekday contract and not a seven-day
contract . . .

For the last twenty-one years Thames has had one high
priority – to sustain and retain its IBA franchise. That is
not a credible business plan for the future because it is only
one of a number of options.

The other prospect is that we might, as an alternative to
bidding for a terrestrial franchise, run a joint operation
perhaps with other companies to put our programmes on
an Astra transponder – though that would depend on the
spread of Astra dishes by the time the decision had to be
made, i.e. the end of 1991. It is an interesting prospect.

The concern about the system of bidding for franchises is
reiterated by other voices. Even where there is no financial
reason for not putting in a bid since the company involved
would – as it believes – be able to raise the money in the City
without difficulty, there are still reservations, expressed by
Brian Tesler.

The problem lies in the method of awarding the
franchises. If it is going to be a tender – a figure written
on a piece of paper in a sealed envelope – we could lose
the franchise by a pound. Someone else could just bid a

pound more. We know the business and the potential of it even if the future is so uncertain, so our bid would be realistic. You cannot compete with people who are prepared not to be realistic but who just want a franchise and don't mind how much they pay for it. Because in comparison with other major industries in this country – conglomerates and multinationals and so on – television companies are small beer. All of us added together . . . are still not much more than half the size in terms of capital value of a single one of the American networks. And therefore a wealthy entrepreneur who wanted the glamour and power of a television franchise would find it very easy to bid a ludicrously high sum for it. That is our concern, because he'd have to recoup his investment somehow and the only way he can do that in the future is by reducing the amount of money he spends on programmes. That is why we don't like the idea, the whole concept, of tendering or auctioning franchises.

Nor is the auction universally welcomed by the advertisers, according to the Director of the Incorporated Society of British Advertisers.

We have some reservations about the auction for ITV channels. We are concerned that it will be possible for too much money to be taken out by the Treasury, by the Government, leaving not enough for good programming. I don't actually think this will happen; but you can write a scenario in which it might happen if the auction process were literally money only. I was very interested in the remark made by the new chairman of the IBA. He said: 'I am interested in the quality of their money.' And the emphasis is on the word quality and not on the word money. Not on the quality of their *money* but on the *quality* of their money. In other words what they are going to do with their money. How secure is it? What are their objectives and intentions? And I think that is quite right . . . We are concerned about the Government's proposal for a levy because if they're going to take an up-front sum from the people who are

successful in getting the franchise, and if there's going to be
a breaking of the monopoly with lots of competition, then
we think it is quite wrong for the Government also to have a
levy on top of that. Because it will again act to reduce the
amount of money that is available for programme-making.
And so we shall be arguing to the Government against the
levy and asking them to be careful about the rules that they
write for how the auction process takes place.

What of the theory that it is in the interests of the viewers and
listeners, which the Government claims to put at the centre of its
broadcasting policy?

I would question that it is in the interests of the viewer
and listener to have a highest bid auction. That may be
the interest of the Treasury and I have no doubt some
politicians could rationalise that if you gave more to the
Treasury that would be passed on to the consumer – but
to pretend that that is in the best interests of
broadcasting is ridiculous.

Nor would the effects of the tendering for programmes be
confined to the ITV companies, in the view of David Plowright.

The highest bid proposed in the White Paper means you
are bidding future profits up front. Inevitably profits
take precedence over programmes; your concentration is
on high ratings, low cost production and the range and
diversity of the present programme schedule is lost. It is
too glib to say that quality or public service
programming will be catered for by the BBC. Faced with
a rampant commercial system, they too would have to
popularise their schedules.
    I remember the BBC, under one of their best Director
Generals, Hugh Carleton Greene, suggesting that if the
BBC dropped below 40 per cent of audience share they
would be beholden to Government of whatever political
persuasion because when they came to seek an increase
in the licence fee the Government could point to their
declining share of audience and deny them an increase
because they were not making the sort of programmes

the public wanted. I think a BBC system faced with a very high intensity of competition from an emerging commercial sector will inevitably have to reduce its aspirations.

Few proposals in the White Paper have aroused such opposition as that concerning the auctioning of the franchises. The unions are united with the employers in their opposition. Thus ACTT, which is naturally worried about the possible effects on its members' employment prospects, takes the view, which is shared by the Secretary General of BETA, that:

> Auctioning to the highest bidder will not necessarily allocate franchises to the companies best qualified to provide a television service and will divert a vast amount of scarce resources away from production. If nonetheless some form of auction is adopted, then the programming promises should be rigorously examined and the final decision should be on the quality of service rather than on the financial bid. There should be full disclosure of information and a requirement for at least the equivalent of original programming as under the present franchises.

Concern over the proposal to auction the franchises for the next contract round in 1992/93 to the highest bidder is shared by the IBA's Director of Television.

> It is a bizarre notion . . . that the 1992/93 change-over will be decided on the highest bid but that thereafter the ITC will have the discretion whether to award the contract without advertisements – without an auction. It seems extraordinary that the present ITV contractors are being punished collectively. They have to go through the auction process – they don't know the scale of bid outside – but thereafter their successors or indeed they themselves if they win will not be subject to this kind of test. They will be able to apply to the Commission and have their franchise extended subject to satisfactory performance. This auction is of a kind which is not present anywhere else in public tendering. If you're tendering for a bridge or a school or a hospital you don't

necessarily have to take the highest tender, you can take into account other factors – the reliability of the track record of the people tendering and so on. Here, as the White Paper says, there is absolutely no discretion once the so-called quality threshold has been gone through. The quality as defined is such that anybody with the meanest intelligence can write a paper that will get them through that. And thereafter if somebody bids £1 more than anybody else they get the contract. No argument. I think that is what our new chairman meant when he talked about the quality of money rather than just the quantity of money.

From the point of view of David Plowright, of Granada Television, there is a need for the new ITC to be clear in its requirements from the franchise-holders in order to keep alive the tradition of public service which transcends purely commercial considerations.

I expect the ITC is going to have some pretty firm ideas about the range and quality of the sort of programmes that will be required of someone applying for a franchise. We would hope that is the case because we are going to do our best over the months of public debate about the White Paper to remind the public at large that their pre-school programmes, their documentary programmes, are all frankly at risk under the current proposals. They will go to the edges of the schedule before they finally fall off the cliff. I'm hopeful that the ITC will, even if it risks duplicating some of the fuddy-duddy rules – as they are now regarded – of the IBA, will have the courage to say that broadcasting is for something other than selling goods.

The Chairman of IBA, who will in due course be the first Chairman of ITC and will therefore preside over the granting of the franchises in 1993, has no qualms about tendering, but is a believer in the 'quality of money'.

I don't believe the Government ever intended to set up a

system where tender touting or spiv bidding could take place; but unfortunately that's what could have happened if you accepted a quality threshold that was full of easy and empty promises. Someone could write for me – as an applicant – a quality threshold and I could then put in a bid. I could get the tender and have no intention of making a programme and sell it on the next day to somebody who would give me a million for my bother. That was never intended, I'm sure, but that's what not looking at the quality threshold but just at the bid meant. This became very apparent to me at the very beginning, which is why on Day One of my appointment I used the phrase 'quality of money'.

Through the years I've seen franchise failures in television and radio and I've been part of helping to salvage them, but the root cause has not been the quality programmes they've promised or tried to make. It has been the lack of money behind them to have the staying power to keep going. TV AM was a classic case. You couldn't have had five more eminent people wanting to put forward a more eminent programme for breakfast. But it collapsed in a very short time because the ideas were there but there was no money base.

So I started off thinking: What on earth happens if somebody puts in a bid that is the highest but doesn't have any money? You've got to have the authority to say No, which starts by saying we've got to look fundamentally at the business plan of the person making the bid. I like the tendering concept because it gets rid of one I don't like – the levy, which is a diktat system. At least the tender, if it gets rid of the levy, says quite clearly what someone is willing to pay to live in this rented accommodation – because that's all they are. There used to be monopoly rented accommodation but the monopoly is fast disappearing so it is just a case of what you are willing to pay for the right to have this house called Thames or LWT.

Having accepted that as not a bad thought, I then said 'Well, if it's a good idea to find out what the licence is worth by the tendering system, is it then reasonable to decide who gets it by the tendering system?' They are two totally separate concepts. We know the value of the licence because of the tender, but how do you decide who should get it? You have then got to look at what I described as 'the quality of money' . . . This fundamental business assessment led me to the conclusion that the 'double envelope' system was very close to what the Government is looking for.

In the first envelope you would put who you are, what you are intending to do, what sort of programmes you think you're going to make for that particular franchise, and what your money base, what your reserves are, and what your talent is. If one takes that first half of the business and, having previously asked the public what they want in the way of regional programmes, one would then let the public comment again on this 'open dossier'. The second and confidential envelope contains the advertising revenue forecast from the programme planned in the area, the profit forecasts, what tax they're going to pay on those profits, and what they're prepared to bid on top of a base price, which we would establish before the tender went out – which is the prime rent for the house – that's the best way of describing it. The bid will be a percentage of your net advertising revenue, not to be paid up front, but to be paid through the years. So you solve the other Government problem in the White Paper – which was the lump sum up-front payment that could drain the whole system and leave nothing to make any programmes at all.

I have also got two merchant banks, which will run in parallel, to assess all those company plans and they'll be assessing the whole 'quality of money' argument just as our broadcasters will be assessing the quality of programmes, because we've got to say 'Will these programmes earn the sort of money people claim?' And people will be rejected or downgraded because they're overstating. There's no point in bidding for the current Granada area and saying 'We can earn that revenue' if you don't have something up to *Coronation Street* in your bid . . .

I believe this is the easiest way to solve the conundrum of

how to keep quality to the fore, how not to drain the system, and how to give the Government the sort of rental money they think they should be getting for this without undermining all that's been achieved in the last thirty-five years.

Once the question of the franchises has been settled there will remain the question of how the contractors awarded the regional franchises for Channel 3 will operate, which they will do in the face of increased competition and a more exacting levy in the form (as the White Paper puts it) of 'a percentage of advertising levy at progressive rates'. The 'positive programme requirements' laid down in the paper are not – 'and need not be' – as extensive as those now governing ITV. They include, however, the requirement, which will for the first time be 'an express statutory requirement', to show regional programming including programmes produced in the regions. This will prevent situations like that which obtained into the Seventies when ATV (then the Midlands contractor) had its offices at Marble Arch and its production studios near London – a situation which the IBA at last stepped in to rectify by instructing the company to move into the region it was ostensibly serving and to have a production centre there.

The Government envisages that Channel 3 will provide the same universal coverage. The important difference will be that the individual companies will in law be 'the broadcasters' and not the ITC, which in this will differ from the present controlling body, the IBA. It follows that the ITC will not have a responsibility for the scheduling or prior clearing of programmes. That responsibility will devolve on to the contractors who will have to decide among themselves 'on commercial grounds' – not, it should be noted, on grounds of public good or the viewers' interests – on any arrangements for networking or syndicating programmes among themselves. If network scheduling (which is a complicated matter and has up to now taken place under the auspices of the Authority) is to take place, there will require to be a networking committee of the ITV

Association; but there will no longer be an umpire to regulate disputes and divergences of interest or to protect local interests against pressures from the metropolitan companies. David Glencross of the IBA (which will by then have been transformed into the ITC) takes the view that there must be some arrangement to provide a basic national service to viewers.

The White Paper doesn't rule out a network, it simply says that it will not be up to the ITC to insist on one or indeed on the particular arrangements that cause one to be formed. I think that the companies will find it in their interests post-1993 to establish a network but it will not in my view be an easy process particularly since the financial burdens placed on the contractors in 1993 – whoever they are – with the levy as well as the auction – are going to be very considerable; but I think again we must argue for the companies as well as the ITC to bring about some new working arrangements. They won't necessarily be the same as the present ones but in the viewers' interest it seems to me that there should be an ITV network which can look the BBC in the face and which can bring to viewers everywhere in the UK the basic network spine of programmes which they've hitherto enjoyed. It would be wrong if viewers in remoter parts of the country or poorer, less populated parts of the country, which didn't generate as much advertising revenue as the major cities, were to be deprived of some of the major network programmes. I mean the whole range – not just factual programmes – I'm talking about major entertainment programmes, sport, everything.

Granada Television in the North-West has always been proud of its regional identity as well as of the important contributions it has made to the ITV network schedules over the years, often displaying considerable independence and a willingness to resist IBA pressures. The Chairman of it's Broadcasting Division wishes to argue 'for a broader definition of regionalism than the one that currently applies to ITV'.

We are the longest serving ITV contractor. We are very
committed to regional broadcasting – and remember that
Independent Television was founded as a genuine
regional system and in a sense complementary to the
BBC because of it. Great centres of broadcasting
excellence were encouraged to develop outside the
South-East. We claim the North-West is one of them.
Obviously there is a duty to cover the region and report
it to itself through your local news and current affairs,
which is endorsed in the White Paper. What is lacking is
a requirement for regional stations to have the same
opportunity as they have had in the past to perform on
the national stage through a network.

Without that requirement there is a danger that the
mainstream provision of network programmes will come
again from the South-East. We will be replaying the
Fifties so far as regionalism is concerned. It would be a
mistake; for an educated democracy is better served by a
broadcasting system which allows Britain to look at
Britain rather than one which gives an exclusive view
from the South-East.

The Chairman of the IBA has what some may feel is a rather
rosy view of the regions.

For all sorts of reasons ITV has been most successful
because it is a regional system. The BBC is the London-
based service, the ITV system is fifteen regions
speaking to each other and offering programmes to the
network based on the regional cultures. Tyne Tees made
a super programme called *Barriers* a few years ago and
eventually it won an international gold award in New
York for the best children's drama. The network enables
the regions to speak to the network and get space to do it
so it seems to me that here's a tremendous pride right
across the country in the fifteen companies plus TV AM.
What is wrong with the regional concept? The answer
has to be nothing other than that some are weaker and
smaller than others.

One of the complaints directed at the ITV network has been that as a monopolistic system it uses a widespread system of subsidies. The Chairman of the IBA denies the charge.

Should they be subsidised? The answer is they're not because straight economics says if you have got 600 transmitters and they earn a million pounds that is all you can pay for them. You can't ask them to pay for the cost of the 600 transmitters – they're there, the money was sunk years ago. It is the earning power of these which counts. For example, Grampian has 8 main transmitters and over 70 relays and Thames and LWT have got 1 main transmitter and about 30 relays. But Thames and LWT account for 27 per cent of the net advertising revenue of the system, therefore Thames and LWT should pay that sort of percentage for their transmission system compared to Grampian. It's just the earning power of the transmitters so there is no subsidy there.

Where I am recommending a sort of subsidy, which may disappear later, is the concept of negative tendering for some smaller regions and instead of saying the rent I expect from you is a million pounds, I say 'You're going to be a caretaker and I will give you a million pounds to run it. Now bid. And you will bid and you might say, 'I am prepared to pay half a million pounds for this franchise.' So the net figure is I give you half a million pounds to run it each year. That gives you a chance to build and survive in this harsh climate. You may be taken over but under the rules I have asked for a moratorium on take-overs for two years, which stops the tout tendering. You can't get a franchise and just sell it straight on, you've got to run it for two years before you can allow it to be taken over. People can't just sit down and say, 'We can save a lot of money that way' because it is very important to the Scottish people.

The White Paper sees the ITC as having a less interventionist role than the IBA. It will no longer have mandatory powers, will not be involved in scheduling, because 'as viewers exercise greater choice there is no longer the same need for quality of service to be prescribed by legislation or regulatory fiat'. Above all, as the Chairman of the IBA stresses, the ITC will no longer be the broadcaster.

The fifteen companies will be the broadcasters. If there are court cases they'll get sued – not the ITC – and they will be expected to exercise their own judgement of what is broadcast within the guidelines of the ITC and probably the Broadcasting Standards Council . . .

A decision has already been taken to put control of advertising back into the hands of the television companies and the IBA will work as an auditor, selecting no more than 15 per cent of the scripts to check in areas of advertising which are known to be more sensitive or complex and obviously dynamite ones where we know there can be trouble will be passed up to us. So you already have change taking place . . . We believe the ITC will not pre-vet any commercials but will draw up and advise on the Code.

There will be less required in terms of minority public service broadcasting from each of the channels because we propose it should be spread. Companies won't be cajoled to add more because they'll know clearly in their contracts what is expected of them in terms of quality – for example, six hours of regional programming. But they'll be watched in terms of maintaining the quality. It will be much more 'You realise that you're in breach of your contract – here is a formal warning' and 'You realise that you've had another warning' leading to what has been dubbed the 'red card' or one of the range of sanctions which will be available to the ITC. But it's not the IBA changing the programmes or making them better – the licensees have to do that themselves because they know they're under threat of perhaps having to apologise publicly or having the contract determined two years early or the ITC saying it will be determined if they haven't improved in a year's time. These are the tough lines on which the ITC will work which the IBA doesn't operate now because it is the broadcaster.

With the exception of the last area it is a lighter touch all through – a lot less regulation – but that is probably a good thing because the whole thing has ossified. The network needs restructuring. We say there has to be a network because otherwise you can't run a high-quality popular schedule. It would all be individual negotiation – fifteen to fifteen – and you'd never get Inspector Morse shown across the whole system – you'd get it on one or two at different times and the advertisers would be annoyed because they wouldn't know when they're going to get the blockbusters with their advertisement matching. We will put in the franchise document: This is the network system you've got to accept; but thereafter it is up to the companies to run it.

A postscript: second thoughts

The White Paper invited comments on its proposals. To judge by a statement made to the House of Commons in June 1989 by the Home Secretary they seem to have concentrated on a number of salient points – chief among them the proposal to award franchises to the highest bidder and the future of Channel 4. The terms of the statement indicate that so many respondents were critical that the Government was forced to have second thoughts. Thus the Home Secretary stated that the Government proposed 'to strengthen the quality threshold by broadcasting the third positive requirement . . . of the Paper' (i.e., the requirement to provide 'a diverse programme service') by laying down that each Channel 3 station should 'provide a reasonable proportion of programmes (in addition to news and current affairs) of high quality'. This was generally seen as little more than a gesture – a form of words; the question of the criteria to be applied and by whom was left unresolved.

On Channel 4 the Home Secretary was more concrete. The Government had decided that

. . . it would not be feasible for Channel 4 to become an independent commercial company competing with the other broadcasters if, as we think essential, it is to retain its remit.

This was a considerable climb-down which recognised that 'the financial outlook for Channel 4 remains uncertain with the prospect of new competition and that a satisfactory return for investors could not easily be achieved'. But the Government did not wish the Channel to be owned by the ITC, which would be responsible for regulating its output. It therefore proposed that Channel 4 should become a public trust licensed by the ITC while continuing to have its special remit. It would be dependent on its own advertising but with a safety net set at 14 per cent per annum of the net advertising revenue of the terrestrial commercial broadcasters. Were the channel's revenue to fall below that figure, the difference would be funded by the ITC through a levy on the Channel 3 companies of up to 2 per cent of net advertising revenue. Complementary scheduling between the channels would be encouraged but not imposed, as would cross-trailing between Channels 3 and 4.

The idea of a public trust had been canvassed by various respondents and in particular by IPPA. The proposals were cautiously welcomed by the main interests concerned. Only time will show whether Channel 4 will be able to be competitive in a fight for advertising and yet avoid modifications of its programme policy.

The Government's other second thoughts – no doubt also reflecting anxieties expressed by the respondents – dealt with broadcasting in the night hours on Channel 3 and with the licensing of Channel 5. In the first case, the White Paper had suggested that the night hours on the channel might be allocated to a separate night hours licence; instead the Government now proposes that they remain with the daytime broadcaster. As for Channel 5, which the White Paper foresaw as being split between two licensees, that would now be allocated under a single licence 'in the light of the start-up costs and the competition [the channel] will face from the established terrestrial channels'.

One other concern had been that over the possibility of take-over bids for franchises, which will no longer be ruled out under the new legislation. In the present financial climate where there are obviously huge sums of money in the economy available for take-overs, the possibility of financial interests with access to such funds taking over from the original franchise-holders is obvious. The Government however made it clear that it does not intend to interfere with market forces.

In line with the same philosophy the Government affirmed that it was not prepared to enforce networking arrangements on the channel saying only that 'basic fair trading laws should ensure that no companies are excluded unfairly from networking arrangements', the stress being typically on 'free access and free competition' rather than on the advantages of networking to the viewing public.

THIRTEEN

The Proliferating Channels

One of the questions left open by the White Paper was how Channel 4 should be funded. The White Paper, as we have seen, pays tribute to the channel's record, one reflection of which has been its success in attracting advertisers. There is therefore in the Government's view a strong case for its being directly funded from its advertising revenue. 'Greater competition between those selling television air time . . . is essential.' This the Paper says is 'a pressing demand from those whose expenditure on advertising has paid for the independent television system'; which brings us back to the advertising lobby.

The options as the White Paper sees them are:

Option 1
There should be a private sector company, selected by competitive tender and licensed by the ITC to provide the service, which – as well as being innovative and experimental – should address a wide range of minority tastes. But there could not in this case be 'an express requirement' to be different from all other services licensed by the ITC for the obvious reason that such a remit would make the channel less competitive with Channels 3 and 5. The channel would be free to sell air time, charge subscriptions or raise funds through sponsorship.

Option 2
The channel could remain a non-profit-making organisation under the ITC, free to raise funds by advertising,
subscription and sponsorship but with a minimum guaranteed income. For example, the ITC could agree with
Government a base-line to which the channel's income
would, if necessary, be made up, drawing on the proceeds
of the competitive tender and the levy.
Option 3
There should be some sort of link between Channels 4 and
5. The channels would then plan their schedules together –
with cross-channel promotion – in order to compete with
Channel 3 and the BBC.

The channel's Chief Executive, Michael Grade, is opposed to
a solution that would make it profit-related.

> We wouldn't benefit from any restructuring that made us
> profit-related, that gave us shareholders, that had us
> competing in the market-place; because what would
> happen is that in order – quite rightly to show a return
> for the capital invested by the shareholders – we would
> have to seek profit and we would have to seek audiences.
> We would have to seek to compete with rather than to
> complement the other channels – and that would be the
> end of the distinctive programme remit of the channel.
> We have an arrangement at the moment that gives us a
> percentage of the ITV advertising revenue in advance
> based on the previous year's performance. That protects
> us from competing in the market-place and enables us,
> since we have secure and adequate funding, to operate
> the remit we currently enjoy.

This fear is echoed by David Plowright of Granada.

> If Channel 4 were to be separated from ITV and had to
> earn its own keep I think we'd all agree that it couldn't
> do so without changing its programme remit. The
> argument has neglected to take account of the fact that
> either ITV is with Channel 4 or it's against it. If it's

against, it is a competitor for revenue. Then Channel 4 loses promotion on ITV worth probably £50 million a year. They have to hire their own sales force, who would encourage the pursuit of ratings, and Channel 4 would move inexorably in the direction of ITV – more of the same instead of more that is different.

The White Paper admits in a moment of candour that if it were 'operated by a private company anxious to maximise profits' this might make it difficult for the channel to live up to its remit to be innovative, adventurous etc. So the subject has been left open and suggestions invited.

One body to take up the question was the eleven-member all-party Home Affairs Committee of the House of Commons which heard evidence from Channel 4, from the IBA and from the ITV Association. Which option would they favour?

As far as Option 1 was concerned, the Committee found that only the evidence submitted by 'those representing the interests of the advertisers', e.g. the Incorporated Society of British Advertisers, were in favour of the channel becoming a private company. Paul Bainsfair of Saatchi & Saatchi states the advertisers' point of view very clearly.

Obviously there are some real breakthroughs [in the White Paper]. One of the proposals is that Channel 4 will be sold separately so that although the audience for the channel is a lot smaller than the audience for the main independent channel there will be some competition. They will be competing with one another for the pounds that are to be spent on the advertising time. So that's good.

In spite of the advertisers' enthusiasm, the Committee dismissed the proposal as 'an unacceptable risk' on the grounds of an inevitable conflict between the interests of the channel and those of the shareholders.

Option 3 was also rejected on the grounds that Channel 5 would take some time after 1993 (if it is indeed launched then) to build up an audience share and profitability. It would be unwise, the Committee decided, 'to expose Channel 4 to the danger of association with a weak partner and to give Channel 5 an inbuilt financial responsibility'.

That left Option 2, which the Committee accepted as the best solution, rejecting in so doing a variant which would have involved the setting up of an independent trust to run the channel. There remained the question of the figure at which the financial guarantee should be set. The subsidy is at present set as a proportion of net advertising revenue (NAR) of the ITV companies. The average for the last five years has been rather over 14 per cent. The Committee accepted 14 per cent of the NAR as 'a safety base line' in the form of a financial guarantee funded by the ITC. If this recommendation is adopted, the Committee's Report concludes, it will not only ensure the future of Channel 4 but will also contribute to the well-being and esteem of independent television as a whole.

It is an important recommendation, which will undoubtedly have much weight when the new Television Bill which will emerge from the White Paper is debated. But there is equally little doubt that the advertising lobby will be working hard to ensure that the final arrangements are favourable to their interests.

The Home Office appears to favour the same approach, although at the time of writing there is still some uncertainty about where it stands on the question. But it is the view of the Chairman of the IBA (ITC to be) that the economic future of Channel 4 is reasonably secure; he is, however, prepared to consider some interesting worst cases.

> Channel 4, I think, is now with the joint selling of advertising [with ITV] more than breaking even – that includes paying for transmitters.
>
> What it mustn't become is the dumping ground for things others don't want to do. It has always been a channel designed to do things that others don't do – or haven't thought of doing – not don't want to do. But it has become a little bit of a dumping ground. When

schools programmes moved from Channel 3 to Channel 4 that was really putting a commercial loser on to Channel 4 and freeing time to make more money on Channel 3. I don't want to see that happen. We'll do our best to ensure it doesn't.

The future arrangements we support are in many respects more secure than the option of being tied to Channel 3, for if Channel 3 does have a horrendous collapse it could take Channel 4 down with it. But Channel 4 with a special fall-back position guaranteed by the Government if they can raise sufficient revenue through their own advertising sales is another matter. A guaranteed fall-back of 14 per cent of total Net Advertising Revenue (NAR) is what they have asked for to carry out their remit of going for the 10 to 12 per cent ratings and to produce all these minority programmes in a way that has been so successful. It has been a major success and I don't see why it shouldn't be in the future. It is somewhat cossetted by what has been structured for it, if you think about it. It will be a national network. It can sell its own air time nationally.

But there is a coda to this eulogy which may sound ominous to the advocates of experiment and innovation, raising as it does the bogey of 'programmes that nobody watches' and memories from the early days of Channel 4 of audience research pundits appearing on air to demonstrate that 250,000 viewers was a ridiculously small audience for any programme: only a quarter of a million people. The Chairman of the IBA thinks Channel 4 is going to have to question its programme policy.

Minority programming is one thing – programming, that is, for a small number of people – but you've really got to question if you make programmes that nobody watches. Is that a result at all? So Channel 4 should not always have to go for programming that gets advertising in but has to get ratings, otherwise it is not doing its job. That job is to improve the market and if certain programmes aren't viewed, having been marketed, policy must change. It's not a channel just to make programmes that aren't to be seen. That's what television is about. It's there to be viewed. So they've really got to look, I think, at some of the programming as to why some of it is made. It could be held to be very worthy – but one of the phrases about Channel 4 is 'It is more talked about than seen' and we want it to be more seen than talked about. So I am confident about its future.

Channels 5 and 6

Where the new Channel 5 is concerned, the Government believes that the licence should be national in scope and not have regional obligations. However, it does propose that 'the Channel could be split up in time into two or more different licences covering different parts of the day and night'. They see good cause for such segmentation 'which will provide competition and enhance diversity' – quite how is not spelt out. Although the new channel is due to come onstream in 1993 there is little discussion of its role in the spectrum of British broadcasting. The IBA's Director of Television takes the view that it should be a national channel.

> I think the best and most practical solution is to have the fifth channel merely as a national channel although we know – currently anyway – that the technology suggests we could only get 70 per cent coverage in large parts of the South. London, I think, would not be covered. Given that ITV is already a regional-based system, that the technology allows us – though the economics are by no means certain – to have point-to-point and local television through MVDS, to have another locally or regionally based service is probably not a very good idea. As for Channel 6, if we ever get as far as that, who knows? That might be organised on a regional basis but not necessarily the same regional basis as the existing services.

If Channel 5 is not to have universal coverage but nevertheless to be national in scope, how should it be run and with what policies? The British Film Institute in its submission to the Home Secretary in response to the White Paper had the following suggestions.

There may be a case, since there may be difficulties in getting the new channel accepted, for retaining the channel as one franchise initially.

Given the geographical spread of the new channel there is a good case to be made for it to be required to be based away from London. This would mean that there would be a desirable development of production facilities outside the London area. It would also have the effect of letting a national channel emerge from a genuinely regional position.

Given that Channel 5 will be perhaps the last national terrestrial channel to be introduced, we would wish to see maximum discussion before the franchise is allocated . . . the following programme strands should be given priority when the franchise applications are being considered:
Open University and Open College programmes;
children's programmes;
an Arts channel;
parliamentary programmes;
documentary programmes.

These are very laudable suggestions and it was right to make them, to have them on the record. Past experience, however, suggests that the Government is more likely to give ear to the advertisers, who naturally are for a proliferation of channels.

We're in favour of a fifth channel. We're in favour of a sixth channel and – if there's room in the spectrum – of a seventh channel because we believe that terrestrial programming and terrestrial stations do have a much better chance of succeeding than satellites. Satellites do require a certain kind of commitment on the part of the viewer. You've got to buy a dish – you've got to fit into that whole framework, whereas a terrestrial channel like Channel 5 will be available to about 70 per cent of viewers quite quickly and a sixth channel probably to 50 per cent of viewers. We argued, when we were lobbying the Government in favour of local television, that you could have a Manchester station and a Liverpool station, instead of only Granada covering that whole area. We'd like to see a Birmingham station and a Coventry station and whatever instead of one company covering all of the Midlands. So we should like to see more choice of the framework but also more choice of the kind of owner providing programmes to the viewers.

Actually we proposed a fifth channel that was local and the Government said No, we don't think we'll do that but maybe we'll do it in a different way . . . There's a limit to the amount you can go on arguing. They've said they'll provide a fifth channel and they will make it competitive and it will be funded by advertising. So we're pretty happy – but we still would like local television . . . We don't want that to be dropped.

The Broadcasting Standards Council

Apart from coming to terms with the various structural and administrative changes envisaged in the White Paper, the broadcasters are going to have to reckon with the Broadcasting Standards Council, which is already in existence and will in due course become a statutory body with no strong sanctions standing alongside ITC and the BBC. It is certainly not what the radicals of the Sixties had in mind when they called for a court of appeal and arbitration which would represent the public and those who worked in broadcasting. Indeed one obvious question is how representative of the public the Council will be. Janet Street-Porter expresses the kind of doubts felt in the television industry on this score.

The setting up of a body that would look at various standards of taste and decency was something we'd been expecting and some people have reacted in a very kind of paranoid way. But I used to work in commercial television with the IBA where I felt there was a very, very grey area. This area of what is offensive is a very grey area. And I do think you have to be accountable to your viewers, your consumers. So long as the body that is going to reflect the consumers' concerns is truly representative of the consumers then I don't have a problem with it. Where I have a problem is if the body is made up of the time-serving old farts who'd be on all the other kinds of quangoes in this country. So what one hopes is that the people who are on the Standards Council are a cross-section of people who truly reflect the diversity of the audience.

Past experience of the composition of such bodies (heavily reliant on the list of the 'great and good') makes this plea sound utopian. Others in the broadcasting industry have doubts about the need for such a body. Melvyn Bragg believes the Government is 'in the jaws of a contradiction'.

It wants to regulate more on the one hand and it wants to deregulate on the other hand. Until that's resolved – and I don't see that it can be resolved – what is going to happen is that one of these forces has to win. I don't think Lord Rees-Mogg is going to make an unfree Britain. I think the concerns he has are about overseas material coming in. I think Mrs Thatcher is worried about soft porn channels coming in. And hard violence channels. I think that's a real concern – although perhaps not as big a concern as they think it is. I don't think there's any real danger yet. And I don't see Rees-Mogg as a dangerous man. Not at all. I think the difficult thing about the Broadcasting Standards Council is the fact that it is yet another body. We've got lots of bodies. We've got the IBA. We've got our own system within LWT. The BBC have got the Board of Governors. We've got the law. These programmes that we make go through enough hoops already.

Bragg is not alone in taking up that position.

It always seemed to me to be unnecessary. I suppose it was an appointment made politically because people were upset with the IBA. Now we are going to have an ITC as well as a Broadcasting Standards Council I suppose they will have to try and find some way of working together but frankly I don't see it as being of major significance. All right, you've probably got to have a Standards Council there to protect against some sort of total attitude towards sex and violence on the screen but I really don't think that this country is going to go down that path. I suspect that before we get to that a compromise will have been reached in the public debate about the White Paper, and that we will finish up with a regulatory system, which isn't too different from what it has been in the past.

That is the view of David Elstein of Thames Television. how does Lord Rees-Mogg, the Chairman of the Council, see his task?

We are preparing the code ourselves but obviously with a great deal of consultation with the existing regulatory authorities – with the BBC, with the IBA and with broadcasters and other interested people. When the Council is operating the code we shall be responsible for monitoring the broadcasting that is taking place in the UK – principally of course television. And discussing with broadcasters and with the regulatory authorities developments in television and, of course, breaches of the code if they occur. We don't have regulatory powers – that is to say, we can't stop anybody broadcasting anything. We can't make them broadcast anything though we have the power – not very important, in my view – to make them broadcast adjudications we have reached. But we have a general responsibility for laying down – and then hopefully seeing that they're maintained – standards of taste and decency but also, more importantly, questions of extreme violence and pornography.

The appointment of an ex-editor of *The Times* and ex-deputy chairman of the BBC with the reputation of not being exactly in the vanguard of liberalism aroused the worst fears among broadcasters. They were somewhat reassured by the fact that he has appointed as Director of the Council, Colin Shaw, an executive with long experience in both the BBC and the IBA, who is well aware that the problem of applying codes to what is shown or said on television is a difficult one. It is complicated by the fact that, as the Council points out, 'the presence in the home of broadcast programmes, cable services or videos, is for many people one of trust, with the programme-maker expected to observe certain conventions'. The Council is going to have the difficult task of reconciling the realities of our society in terms of its violence of actions and words with the desire many people have to shelter themselves and their families from representations of that violence. They have also to confront what may be the deeply-held belief of directors and writers that to be truthful about the nature of society is a duty.

The proposals put out for discussion by the Council were on the face of it not much different from the codes in use with the BBC and the IBA. They contain unexceptionable concerns about the stereotyping of the aged and of minority groups, the use of words which have racist overtones, the exploitation of sex, and violence – in particular violence against women.

The Chairman of the Council – he is talking about films, but his remarks hold good for television – finds one thing self-evident: 'the real seriousness of the issue of sadistic attitudes towards women'.

> It is when you get sex and violence coming together, when you get films which are made with a view to meeting a taste for the humiliation and mutilation of women, that you get material which I think is extremely repulsive to view . . . You get a sort of lingering over rape scenes . . . but you also can see who this is aimed at, what is the audience, which is people who have this sort of attitude. It is feeding it, and it must be reinforcing it, must be tending to build it up.

What has alarmed some broadcasters, however, is the suggestion that the Council will apply its rules on violence and good taste to news and current affairs as well as to entertainment, drama and films. This is not to say that newsfilm and documentary footage do not present problems of taste and decency; no one who has worked in these areas of television can be unaware of the difficult decisions that have to be taken about what to show and when to cut. But we live in a violent and brutal age and that violence and brutality must be reflected on our screens if we are not to be presented with a sanitised version of our own and other societies. Would good taste and decency have prevented the important documentary evidence of atrocities in Vietnam – including the shooting of a Vietcong prisoner by a Vietnamese commander – or in more recent times, the shooting of prisoners in cold blood by the Afghani mujaheddin, the Protestant terrorist throwing hand-grenades at a Republican funeral and the frightening scenes when two British soldiers were shown being captured prior to being lynched?

The ITC's concentration on the images shown has been rightly criticised by programme-makers on the grounds that images are not shown in isolation; they appear in the context of other images and are accompanied by speech which supplies a commentary, offers an explanation or a judgement. In other words, they are mediated. At another point in its proposals the Council is in danger of committing the converse error of considering words divorced from the images that accompany them. It is true that the British, who are notoriously given to cursing and swearing, are liable to be shocked when the patterns of their everyday speech are realistically reproduced; but it seems excessive to propose that the use of 'fuck' (one of the most commonly used expletives) and its derivatives should be permitted only after reference to the most senior levels of management. 'The abusive use of any of the synonyms for the female genital organs' is rightly condemned but again reference up is called for. What producers fear is that reference up – usually a laborious process – frequently leads the authorities (as might be the Board of Governors of the BBC) to play safe, to avoid controversy.

Such fears may have been to some extent allayed by the reaction of Lord Rees-Mogg to the attitudes expressed to him in the course of consultations with viewers. He is reported as saying, after criticising the press for underrating the quality of judgement of the British public, that the adult public wants to be told the truth in drama and news programmes.

Worries remain, however, because of rumours that the

Broadcasting Standards Council may wish to preview programmes – which, apart from anything else, is a mammoth job for which it does not seem to be staffed. The other cause for concern is the climate in which, as things stand, the Council must work. Too easily in a moral and political climate like today's when the Prime Minister is prepared to lead a moral crusade to clean up the media rather as she cleans up the parks, 'good taste and decency' can become a cloak for political censorship. (The appointment by the Government of Lord Chalfont, a right-wing peer of very strong views on the limits that must be set to journalistic inquiry, to be Deputy Chairman of the IBA (soon to become the ITC) is symptomatic of that climate.) Will pressures for censorship and self-censorship increase? Codes, however liberal-sounding, have to be interpreted. The nature and liberality of the interpretation is what matters.

Since under the new dispensation the individual contractors will be the broadcasters and not the ITC, the onus of supervising programmes with an eye on the ITC will fall on the ITV companies. David Glencross at the IBA thinks it will place far more responsibility on the ITV companies.

> Until now [they] have been able to look to the IBA for
> protection when they have been transmitting
> controversial programmes. They'll have to take those
> decisions themselves and stand the racket afterwards.
> They won't be able to say to their critics, 'Well, the IBA
> said it was all right, therefore it must have been all
> right.' And I just wonder in the so-called brave new
> world how many ITV companies will actually be
> prepared to stand up editorially when the going gets
> tough. I think that some of them will not be. Some will –
> but it depends who gets the contracts in 1993 and since
> the contracts (according to present plans) are going to be
> awarded purely on the basis of who's got the ability to
> pay and who will bid most after a quality threshold
> which is pretty low, then it seems to me that the people
> prepared to bid the most money are not necessarily the

ones who have the interests either of programmes generally or of journalism at heart.

There might, if he is right, be a return to the bad old custom which obtained in one London company in the Sixties of having a company censor with little understanding of television and film practices who attempted to dictate how film should be cut and what might or might not be said in a documentary.

Others take a more relaxed view of the Council. One of them is the Chairman of the IBA.

> The Broadcasting Standards Council has basically taken the BBC and IBA standards and had a good look at them and put them together. They're a bit more wordy but they're about the same, which shouldn't surprise you as the chap who wrote the IBA's was also the Secretary of the BBC and is now Director of the Council. It seems to me that when the ITC advertises the franchises it would pin to each franchise the BSC's guidelines on taste, decency and all the things that are written up – and that is it. The Council, if they feel somebody isn't observing them, is likely to tell us and to tell them and we are expected either to agree or not and if we feel they're in breach to give them warning and ask them to improve. So we become, I suppose, very much the judge, with the Broadcasting Council the prosecution service, and the broadcaster the defendant.

The prospect is also taken calmly by some broadcasters, of whom David Elstein is one.

> The Council is still taking shape and all that one hears is that its code of practice is not going to be significantly different from the IBA's code of practice which is pretty stringent and therefore in practical terms it would be hard to imagine what difference in our output would be detectable. I asked the BSC to tell me what we transmitted in the past that they wouldn't have allowed and I've yet to hear of any single programme that ITV has transmitted that it would not have allowed . . . But

it would be administratively irritating if they became a previewing organisation because there's so much that can be previewed. Where do you stop? And what do we do then with our own internal previewing function? Do we abandon it and substitute the BSC's judgement or what? At the moment if we've got any problems with a programme, have any anxieties about it, we consult the IBA, but the IBA doesn't, except in the most unusual circumstances, require sight of a programme before it's transmitted. So I don't spend much of my time worrying about the BSC.

He may be reassured by the account Rees-Mogg gives of the difficulty of coming to decisions over questions of taste.

You view something and you think 'Well, that's rude and will offend some people but it's not serious and it's not got anything in it which feels vicious or wrong' and you're not really in much doubt about that decision. You view something else and you see that really it is very horrible, anti-human and degrading and corrupting, in a way which is totally unacceptable on the mass media. And you're not in much doubt about that. And then of course you get, absolutely inevitably, a number of things which are on the borderline – which sensible and experienced people would actually take different views about which category they came into.

What he describes here is the classic dilemma of the regulators who clearly do not make their judgements in a vacuum but on the basis of certain assumptions about the nature of society, of what is good and what is bad, about morality and the public good. In a society – like our own – which is deeply divided there is unlikely to be a consensual backing for the Council's ruling. What is one person's sense is another person's unreason. It all depends on the experience of life, on the social and class background of those who are called upon to make the judgements.

From an institutional point of view the Council presents a problem probably not envisaged by the Government. The chief of these is the question whether it might not begin to take on some of the functions up till now discharged by the IBA and become in some ways a regulatory body; which is presumably the last thing Mrs Thatcher had in mind when she appointed Lord Rees-Mogg.

FIFTEEN

The Advertising Lobby Again

If in the run-up to the White Paper the advertising lobby used less flamboyant methods than it did in 1954 when campaigning for the inauguration of commercial television, its efforts have nevertheless been highly effective. A leading role was played by the Incorporated Society of British Advertisers (ISBA), which acts as the channel between advertising interests and the Government, the civil service and broadcasting organisations. The ISBA's complaint, as its Director explains, was that it had insufficient outlets for advertising on the television screens.

> In television in Britain we have not enough channels for companies to buy advertising time because previous governments have decided that they knew best how many television channels there should be and they have prevented more channels from being launched. We believe that that is a thoroughly unsatisfactory state of affairs. It has been unsatisfactory for some years and the Government, I am glad to say, has now recognised that it is so – that they have no business interfering with the supply of television programmes to viewers or for that matter to advertisers. Indeed they have recognised that with the advent of satellite television they couldn't prevent it anyway . . . What we have seen for the best part of the last ten years is that the costs of producing programmes and the costs of advertising on them have gone to a ridiculously high level – far higher than in most other countries. And therefore the viewer has had poor

value. They have been prevented from getting new channels and we, the advertisers, have had poor value; we have had to pay very high prices to a series of monopoly services. The Government has recognised that this is not in the interest of free trade; it is not in the interest of the viewer and therefore they determined to change it. We have played a part in persuading the Government that this is the case, but above all the unsatisfactory nature of the present position has been the main factor in getting them to see what needed to be changed.

There is, however, a question. If the system the Government is proposing is adopted, will there be enough advertising revenue to go round? David Wheeler the Director of the Institute of Practitioners in Advertising has few doubts.

I think the scope for more advertising to finance more television channels is very considerable. We know that many people would like to get on to television for their advertising but simply cannot either because it is too expensive or because there is simply not enough space on television. The more people who come in, the higher the price goes because there is a monopoly and restricted supply. When we have a greater supply and competing channels then the price will stabilise. My personal opinion is that it will not significantly come down but it will be more efficient because the programming will be better targeted to different categories of viewers.

The concept of targeting – which means, in fact, the breaking up of the mass audiences of the past into groups and categories which can be identified in terms of incomes and spending power – is (as we shall see later) a crucial determinant of advertisers' broadcasting strategies.

But what of the complaint that up till now there has been too little advertising space? Restrictions on advertising go back to the Television Act 1954 and were motivated by the fear that commercial television in Britain might follow the American pattern. There commercial breaks are inserted in clusters with little regard to programme considerations. For virtually the whole of the 33 years of ITV's existence the amount of advertising was set at 6 minutes in the hour with a normal maximum in an hour of 7 minutes. In 1988, however, as its Controller of Advertising explains, the average minutage was increased by the IBA to 7 minutes in the hour and a maximum of 7½ minutes in peak time.

> The 7½ minutes in peak time followed representations from the advertising industry who were concerned about airtime inflation. The demand for television advertising was rising inexorably – it is driven by consumer expenditure and the economy – and as the economy kept expanding there is more and more advertising budget chasing the same amount of advertising opportunity.

But the dissatisfactions of the advertisers are focused not only on what they regard as inadequate air time but on the structure of the ITV network itself, which they see as being (from their point of view) an unsatisfactory monopoly controlling commercial access to the television screen. Now that monopoly will be broken with the opening up of a new commercial television channel (Channel 5) and with the proposal to make Channel 4 self-financing. Broadly speaking, they are pleased with the White Paper (which has been described as an advertisers' charter), although John Blakemore of Ogilvy & Mather no doubt speaks for others when he expresses one great regret.

> It has introduced competition into the airtime market and there are a number of sales practices that go with a monopoly market that are very frustrating, very restrictive, and these will disappear, hopefully, post 1993. So broadly we are happy with the White Paper. The one thing we really, really would have liked to have seen – it does seem a lost cause – is advertising of some form or another on the BBC.

A rich prize – one which the reactions of Paul Bainsfair leads one to think they may wish to have a second shot at when the Charter comes up for renewal.

We are broadly excited about it [the White Paper]. I say that with a qualification because we were very active a couple of years back – round about 1985 – when there was a tremendous amount of lobbying going on to encourage the Government to consider taking advertising to fund the BBC television service, and we were very active – in fact leading the lobby pro advertising for the BBC. And certainly we feel, still feel, that that would have been a much more significant breakthrough from our perspective as advertisers in terms of what it meant for our business and that's very simply because, given the way the independent television service is structured over here, it is virtually a monopoly in terms of selling television time.

But the general reaction is positive, as John Blakemore of Ogilvy & Mather makes clear. There have, in his words, been 'some real breakthroughs'.

Obviously the advent of more channels is tremendously good news because more choice for us means two things. It probably means that the cost per thousand will fall over time because quite simply it is like having two grocers in a street rather than one . . . And the other thing that it will lead to is far greater targeting. What I mean by that is . . . that when we have a far greater array of programming through the new channels there is likely to be much more opportunity for me to buy at a lower cost programmes or ads in programmes that are targeted at a group of people. So there will always be wastage but it means I can reach the same number of people I wanted to reach in the beginning at a fraction of the cost. And I can do it more often with the money I have available to me and indeed the environmental quality of the advertising *vis-à-vis* the programming is likely to be more similar.

The proposal that Channel 4 should sell its own advertising instead of relying on the ITV companies is naturally welcomed by the Institute of Practitioners in Advertising (IPA) because it opens up the market.

> We have argued from the beginning that it should be marketed and sold separately and that it was a mistake not to. I'm glad to see that the White Paper has now at last reopened that particular debate. It has been a major achievement on behalf of the IPA to get that point across. Drawing an analogy from the press, had Channel 4 properly marketed its special characteristics it would have sold its air time at a premium. The reality is that it is being sold at a discount, which is absurd.

There are some reservations about Channel 5, which the White Paper states will be 'free to determine its own mix of advertising and subscription', but which, as we have seen, will not be able to achieve universal coverage.

It will, however, be some time after the new dispensation is in operation before the advertisers will be able to see clearly 'where the profits are going to be'. There are problems about ITV – what will become Channel 3 – which is described dismissively as having 'an old down-market audience'. Yet in the uncertain period before the dust has settled there may be advantages in sticking with it. Such at least is the opinion of Paul Bainsfair of Saatchi & Saatchi.

> My initial feeling is that despite the levy implications Channel 3 is still something to look at but you have to look at it very carefully and very seriously because if the auction and levy proposals go through there's unlikely to be much profit there . . . The great advantage of Channel 3 is that it has got its distribution – 98 per cent of homes have got that Channel 3 button. Channel 5 is worth looking at – again because it is national but it is going to be segmented in programme terms and it is going to be some time before it gets good distribution so clearly some time before it makes profits.

If one reason why the advertisers have pressed for an increase in the number of television channels has been the desire to break ITV's monopoly control of advertising, another very powerful motive is that the advertisers have come round to the view that it is advantageous for them and their selling strategies to attempt to fragment the audience. At one time it was the mass audience that television could deliver – audiences of ten to twenty million for popular programmes – that attracted advertisers; now they have had second thoughts, become in their terms more sophisticated in their approach to audiences.

> At the moment television broadly speaking – especially on BBC1 and ITV – is a mass audience vehicle. You get lots of everybody for any programme you care to mention. With the introduction of the new channels and also with the satellites we will go from effectively four channels up to twenty or more in a relatively short space of time. That will mean that the audience are after tight core groups. For example, with Ford Granada we are trying to reach AB businessmen – for obvious reasons. At the moment even if I buy *News at Ten* I've got to buy a lot of women – a lot of housewives – and a lot of C2, D, E men. So there is a lot of wastage. Now hopefully with the fragmentation of the media that wastage will reduce. I'm personally not convinced that the changes will result in the absolute cost of air time going down, if you are after select target groups then Yes, because there will be less wastage. I think the prices might go down but not necessarily if you are after a mass audience, i.e. all housewives or all adults or all men and all women . . .

The way in which this executive from Ogilvy & Mather considers audiences has little in common with the concerns that inspire the philosophy of public service. Universality and availability of programmes or social function are not important in a deregulated, profit-led system. But the advertisers are quick to protest that they have the good of broadcasters and of programmes at heart. Here is the Director General of the IPA:

The most important people in television are the viewers
and if the viewers like programmes they will watch them
and we shall buy time between them. If viewers don't
like programmes they won't watch them. Therefore the
viewers need more choice and the growth of the use of
VCR's in this country demonstrates that many people
were not satisfied with what's on tonight. It is quite clear
from the research that has been done over the years that
the range and choice of programmes – good as it may be
by some standards – is nothing like as good as viewers
would wish. Young viewers are certainly not provided
with as much choice as they would like. Many of the
up-market viewers do not get much choice – particularly
in commercial television . . . More competing channels
will undoubtedly mean that there is more for you and for
me and for everybody else to choose from. Now that will
be good for viewers. It will incidentally be good for
programme-makers because many more producers,
writers, directors, actors, performers will have the
opportunity to be put on the air and it will be good for
advertisers.

Or again, the Incorporated Society of British Advertisers:

Oddly enough, the demand we have been making
consistently over the last five years and the pressure we
have put on the IBA and the programming companies is
towards *raising* the quality of programmes. It is an
absolute myth the idea that what advertisers want, and
where the advertising money goes, is towards the lowest
common denominator. In fact where advertising money
is increasingly going – as is demonstrated in other media
– is towards the premium end of the market. That is
towards premium audiences. Our concern over ITV is
that over the last few years they have not invested
enough in programming with the result that their
audience has become eroded not only in size but in terms
of quality. It has gone down market and up the geriatric
scale.

And that, of course, is the rub. For if we look at the audience not from a purely commercial point of view as a body of consumers who must be persuaded to watch programmes in order to buy goods (which may or may not be useful or pleasurable) and instead consider them as citizens or as human beings who possibly (to put it no higher) may wish to be informed, entertained and (maybe) educated whatever their purchasing power, then this new strategy raises important questions about the fate of those who are rejected by the advertisers as not worth broadcasting to. The dismissal of the ITV audience as geriatric and down-market raises the question of what programmes will be offered and supported by advertisers for the benefit of those of our fellow-citizens who are labelled C2, D and E – which means the poorest and most disadvantaged among us. If they do not constitute a profitable market, who will perform the public service of entertaining, informing and (even) educating them? It is not a question that is discussed in the White Paper or by the spokesmen for the advertising lobby.

SIXTEEN

The Independents and their Lobby

With the prospect of a sharp increase in terrestrial and satellite channels there is clearly the possibility of increased opportunities for independent production companies who will of course be competing not only with producers in the United States but with others in Europe. In Europe, for example, the European Commission's Media 92 Project is putting together private and public funds in an attempt to establish an independent production network in Europe – in particular it is seeking fiction of quality which 'reflects indigenous qualities, is of interest to the European Community, has a production potential'. It is a laudable attempt to ensure that what the new channels provide is not either a flood of cheap American programmes – of which there are a very large number about – or what has been called *Eurodallas*. It is one, however, of which the IPPA, the Independent Programme Producers Association, is somewhat dismissive.

But there will be competition – not only in the field of plays and narrative – from other quarters as well like Brazil and Japan, which have flourishing production industries. Because television production was considered by the Home Affairs Committee on broadcasting to be 'a major growth area for wealth creation and expansion of employment' it urged the BBC and the ITV companies to fulfil their obligation (imposed on them by Government) to achieve 25 per cent production by independent programme-makers, adding interestingly that they should also 'make deliberate efforts to commission programmes from companies based in all parts of the country'.

In discussing independent production a distinction has to be made between independent producers and freelances, although clearly the categories are not always sharply defined. There have always been freelances in British television, working chiefly as producers, directors, writers, editors and performers; they will continue to find employment in that role. The new phenomenon is that of independent production units, which – as we have seen – were greatly encouraged by Channel 4's policy of having no in-house production, as Michael Grade explains.

> The majority of Channel 4's programmes are supplied by independent producers. Channel 4 has enjoyed a monopoly for four years. That monopoly is about to be broken. We are going to have to be competing with the BBC and ITV for the best of the independent producers, ideas and products. We can't compete with the ITV or even the BBC for money – we get £180 million a year, which is something less than BBC2 and a hell of a lot less than ITV or BBC1. We can't outbid the other channels. What we have to be able to provide is what I call after-sales care on the air for the producers. We have to nurse the shows. We have to have faith in ideas that maybe don't work first time round and stick with them. And even more important, we have to get a reputation for giving fast answers – either Yes or No.

One of the attractions of the growth in independent productions to Gunnar Rugheimer of BSB is cost.

> It is clear that you can produce programmes for a lot less money than the established broadcasters do. There are lots of reasons. First of all, overheads – independents produce programmes a lot cheaper than either BBC or ITV because they haven't got overheads. They don't have the union structure. You can do it a lot cheaper without sacrificing quality.

It is worth remembering in this context what it means when one says that independents have no overheads. It is that they have no liabilities to pay pensions or sick pay or holidays; that if, for instance, a production company has a season of thirteen programmes followed by a break, it will lay off most of its staff during the interval and re-engage them (or not) when the next season comes round. If there is scope for the independents in the expanding market, it may – in Bill Cotton's view – prove to be a high-risk business.

I think that all broadcasters have decided that there's a lot to be gained from fishing in the independent pool. There is talk of 25 per cent which I think most of them will reach. There is no doubt about it, there is not a living for 400 independents . . . But I think there will be a fairly decent living for a fair number of independent operators . . . Everything is in the melting-pot and it is emerging slowly how the independents are going to fit in and on what basis. I mean are they going to fit in by using facilities owned by the broadcasters they are working for? Some of the broadcasters just wish to rent their facilities to anybody simply to make the facilities pay.

An effective lobby was organised – as its Director explains – by the Independent Programme Producers Association, a body which came out of the late Seventies campaign about the shape and mode of functioning of Channel 4.

That debate was concluded in 1979/80 when the Government set up legislation which created a fourth channel with two specific briefs – one, as a publishing channel that would commission its work from others, and secondly, that would have a significant proportion of its work from independent producers. The lobby group had formed around this position and had won. Therefore they felt that they needed an association and in 1982 IPPA was formed and has effectively represented the interests of the independent producers ever since. In UK law we are a trade association which is responsible for negotiating on behalf of independent producers with both trade unions and broadcasters.

After their original success 'in creating Channel 4 as a market-place for independents' the IPPA, as its Director explains, turned its attention to a series of issues that couldn't be accommodated by Channel 4. Chief among these was the demand for a 25 per cent share of production on the BBC and ITV networks.

Frankly there are many more good creative and businesslike producers out there than there are slots on Channel 4 to fill. As we began to see the television market-place changing, independents realised that unless they could get a foothold in existing terrestrial TV, particularly ITV and BBC, we would not be able to face the 1990s as a competitive group. So our access campaign has really been about the fact that the BBC and ITV are, in fact, state monopolies that have decided who will work for them and how often. By persuading the Government to include a quota of 25 per cent before 1992, when the main legislative impact of the post White Paper situation will come into effect, we should be in much better shape competitively to cope with the 1990s in a freer market. We say 'freer' because we don't think there's such a thing as a free market in broadcasting.

The question is whether, in the view of the IPPA, that quota is being fulfilled by the BBC and the ITV companies.

Both networks – BBC1 and 2 and ITV – produce 10,000 hours of originated programming at the moment. So a crude divisor would be 2½ thousand hours equals 25 per cent. The broadcasters have persuaded the Government that news and daily-news-related current affairs programmes should be excluded from that target, so we have downgraded our estimates to about 15,000 hours on each network. Now the BBC have said they intend to reach 600 hours by the year 1991. The Government, through its ministers, have repeatedly said that it expects to see full implementation by 1992. So it is quite clear to us that the BBC, in particular, has no intention of meeting the Government's targets. That leaves us in something of a dilemma. We are very supportive of the overall strategies and structures at the BBC and would not wish to seem to be undermining it. However, we also feel that they are using our best intentions to preserve public service broadcasting against our best commercial interests . . .

The debate will go on about what is good and what is bad, but we feel unless there is external arbitration to the BBC's assertion on cost and quality they will effectively be judge, jury, executioner or whatever in their own court.

The IPPA is somewhat vague about how this arbitration should be conducted and by whom, saying merely that 'fair and impartial monitoring . . . would best be achieved with the appointment of an independent evaluator to oversee independent access to all UK channels'. As the system is organised at the moment, it is difficult to see what body might play this role. The logic of the argument could lead to renewed calls for some sort of over-arching Broadcasting Commission; but that is not envisaged in the White Paper nor is it likely to commend itself to a free-market government. Meanwhile the Director General of the BBC maintains that it is on course for what has been agreed.

We took a specific pragmatic view about independent producers. We had to. It was important that an organisation like the BBC, which had produced everything in-house, took a pragmatic approach in changing and restructuring the BBC to absorb independent producers. We have said, starting with a base of about 1,000 hours, that we will get up to about 600 hours in the commissioning process for production in 1991/2. So we will have 600 hours of independent production by then . . . We will then have a review of the success of that policy in 1991. That review has to be in terms of cost and it has to be in terms of quality. Then

there has to be a serious discussion about what is the next
step forward . . .

If the programmes are costing the licence-payer more
than they would by doing them in-house, or if they are not
producing good programmes of quality, that will force us
to see whether the policies should proceed. I actually think
it will work out all right. If we do move forward at a pace we
can manage – because taking on independents means
actually reducing the infrastructure of the BBC and that's a
large managerial task – then I see no reason why it won't
work.

But there is a view of the situation – one held by Bill Cotton –
which sees the employment of independents as one of the
'biggest hurdles the BBC is going to have to jump' as it
integrates the 25 per cent for independent programme-making
into its output.

I don't think it will be disastrous so long as there is a
proper way of controlling it and making sure these
people are producing popular decent programmes. It
won't be cheap – that's for sure. If it's cheaper it will be
terrible. You only get what you pay for in life . . . The
BBC and ITV have both had in the past – one with a
monopoly of advertising revenue and the other with a
monopoly of the licence fee – a secure financial base from
which they have been able to build a major production
capability of world class. The present policy could just
end up very scrappy . . . As for the idea that they [the
independents] are going to run minority programmes –
well, why would they want to do that? They're not going
to make money out of that. They've been set up to try
and make money. They haven't been set up to extend
broadcasting and they won't. I don't see how they can.

The requirement to employ a large number of independents
and concurrently to cut back on in-house production could
mean that the BBC found itself with surplus studio capacity; but
the Director General of the BBC takes another view based on an
estimate of production capacity which appears to overlook the

emergence of new studios – there is already a large independent studio in Glasgow, for example, and various teaching establishments like polytechnics throughout the country have studio capacity and/or facilities which they are anxious to offer for hire and indeed are already offering.

> There are no independent studios really available. There are none outside London. They don't exist, so independents making programmes outside London have the choice of using the ITV studios or BBC studios and I would see independent producers coming in and utilising BBC resources – particularly in a regional context . . . I personally think there will never be large-scale studio or outside broadcast resources available in the independent sector, because they are too capital-intensive and I doubt very much whether anybody will invest in them . . . We shall certainly, over the next few years, be closing down some of our activities; but at the end of the day the BBC will still have a very large studio and outside broadcast base. The independent facilities are likely to be in the more fashionable areas of post-production and video effects and graphics where facility houses with rapid investment policies can be quite appropriate for the broadcasters to use.

The BBC's attitude is one the IPPA dismisses an 'an old-style British establishment trick'.

> They know perfectly well that many people inside broadcasting got their first starts in the BBC. There's an immense sense of loyalty to one of the best broadcasting systems in the world whatever our personal grievance might be with them. We believe – as the Government does – that they are the cornerstone of a much more complex future for broadcasting. And therefore we will do our very best not to destabilise the system. However, we argue that the management discipline and the costing and resources independent producers can bring to the BBC would do two things. One, we would creatively enrich by bringing a diversity of independent talents to

bear, but secondly, some of our business methodologies and our cleaner union agreements would greatly benefit the BBC. I have the vision . . . that the BBC and many senior ITV executives, who have complained about the 25 per cent being imposed on them, privately as managers welcome it . . . In a sense, I think they are playing their cards two ways. They're saying to the independents, 'Come on, boys, we're doing the best we can, don't rock the boat,' and, on the other hand, they're going back and having internal meetings saying, 'Hey, you guys, we have to change, the independents are coming – we've got to clean our act up, we have to be more professional, we have to cut costs and that means there's going to be some hard decisions to be made'. Our dilemma is that we believe in a mixed broadcasting economy . . . So we have, if you like, both a business interest and also a wider broadcasting commitment.

Not everyone who has seen some of the independent companies at work would unreservedly subscribe to this account of them as being necessarily highly cost-effective, economical, 'slim'.

The situation with the ITV companies is, the IPPA's Director admits, more complex than that with the BBC.

Effectively the IBA, soon to be abolished because it has met with disfavour from this government, has been effectively co-opted by the individual ITV companies on a number of issues including this one. What we can see is a tendency that the number of hours being commissioned by the ITV network as a whole . . . is somewhat nearer the target. We don't know the exact figure because – to use a slang expression – the IBA have done a 'snow job' on us and are making exaggerated claims . . .

A second motive for the Government's championing of the independents is linked to the conviction – not borne out by a report by the Monopolies Commission – that the television industry is the victim of restrictive labour practices which the independents might help to abolish. The Government's motives are not necessarily shared by all the independents; but their relationship with the unions has in the past sometimes been a difficult one. Many years ago, however, the ACTT recognised that freelances were inevitable in many branches of the film and television industry and came to support and organise them; but independent producers are in union terms more questionable: because some employers welcome them; because they could be used to undercut wages and conditions; because in union politics they have often represented a right-wing element and have on occasion led the fight against such union policies as a ban on working in South Africa. The reaction of Alan Sapper, General Secretary of the ACTT, is sharp.

> The independents – through the IPPA – are willing allies of the Government in trying to get their programmes on mainstream television. IPPA believes that their present membership will be the independent production suppliers of a new Europe but they won't be. Because the Berlusconis, the Schmidts, the Murdochs, the Maxwells, are already setting up their own independent production units, sales organisations and purchasing organisations too. They have bought up massive libraries in the States and now in Japan, and these are the programmes which are going to be part of the independent input into mainstream broadcasting. Secondly, the independents' idea was to get their programmes on BBC and ITV as they knew it; but BBC and ITV won't be as they knew it. There won't be a market-place for their product even if they could get the money for it.

That view is shared by Tony Hearn, the Secretary General of the other broadcasting union, BETA.

> I certainly think one element in the Government's strategy over the last four or five years is to say that the BBC and ITV have got to use 25 per cent or more of independent production. I think they see that – from our

point of view – as destroying organised trade unions in the big in-house areas.

How successful has the strategy been?

We have agreements that apply to all independent productions in this country – so we are fully and 100 per cent organised in this area. The Government didn't understand that.

The counter-strategy he sees as lying in strengthening union clout by amalgamations between unions engaged in broadcasting.

My union on its own can't cope with these problems. What we try to do therefore is rationalise the trade union structure in the industry by a process of amalgamation with the two or three unions which are key unions in the industry and use our resources to try and preserve some kind of organised basis of opposition to what the Government intends . . . [We] will not look with a benevolent eye on an extension of independent productions and will therefore try to oppose one that kills in-house production. But since the independents exist, yes, we will organise our members in the independent companies.

There are other concerns about the proliferation of independents. One is that the severe erosion of in-house production may in the long run have an adverse effect on the quality of programmes and the possibility of fostering creativity. The intense competition which is bound to arise between producers will militate against the security, the ability to take risks, to allow time for projects (and people) to ripen, which in-house production provides and which, in the climate of intense competition, may be dismissed as an expensive luxury. The argument was developed in *Broadcast* by Richard Patterson of the British Film Institute.

The BBC's vast resources, human and financial, are allocated within a framework established over many

years. They provide an enormous programme production
factory which turns out a wide range of programming –
popular serialised product alongside bespoke
programming commissioned for specific cultural reasons
or to serve particular audiences . . . Commissioning takes
place in close proximity to production, allowing flexibility
for staff and resources not possible to commission-only
operations – one of the problems Channel 4 faces in its
relationship with independent suppliers.

The ITV companies, the argument continues, have 'evolved
as a variant of this vertically integrated model' with considerable
capital assets and adequate staff to maintain the potential for
innovation. They have provided a creative environment in
which there is space for risk-taking alongside the certainties of
profitability. The Government's desire to demolish the vertically integrated structures in the interests of competition may
have negative results. 'The critical mass of development staff
could be endangered as the companies fracture and the creation
of cost centres divides programme-makers from facilities and
sales.'

Should the ITV companies – as is possible if they do not
succeed in their bids for their franchises – live on after 1993 as
production organisations alone, there would be a danger of
breaking the creative nexus linking commissioning with the
impetus to innovate and the all-important in-house independence. 'The destruction of the ITV system could undermine
the creative vitality of the constituent production companies. It
would orientate programming to profitability with notions of
culture abandoned before those of market efficiency.'

There remains the question how the independent market will
develop as the new system begins to function. Already there is
evidence that Channel 4 has begun a system of sub-contracting,
giving a number of programme slots to a large independent
production set-up and allowing it to sub-contract a certain
number of them. The practice – according to Bob Hunter of
BSB – is likely to become more common.

> We have decided to be publishers of programmes rather than producers of programmes. Rather than have lots of small independent companies making programming we have main or prime contractors and they can sub-contract to smaller contractors.

The Chairman of the IBA for his part points to a curiously uncertain future.

> We saw a large role for the independents from the beginning [of Channel 4] and it has been superb. It has spawned a totally independent sector and all sorts of good things have come out of it. However, the distinction is probably going to disappear.

The Government, he believes, will go on talking about the 25 per cent quota; but it will become increasingly difficult to define who is and is not an 'independent'. Suppose the companies who are awarded the Channel 3 franchises decide to become 'publisher contractors' and make programmes for Channel 4: they will then be themselves 'independents'. In other words, very large production units, based possibly on the present Channel 3 contractors, may come into the market-place to compete with the 'independents' who back in the Seventies founded the IPPA and who will then find themselves playing in a very different league.

SEVENTEEN

ET – Extraterrestrial Television

It is inevitable that satellite broadcasting is being recommended ('sold') in advertising terms. The chief benefit of the pro- gramming policy that has been adopted is stated to be that programmes can be targeted on specific groups. These groups are described as belonging to the economic categories current in advertising discourse.

Thus BSB (British Satellite Broadcasting) believes it can tap a demand for greater choice among women, younger adults and ABC1 men – that is, men who top the scale of disposable income. Sky Television 'will attract and hold on to specific audiences *and* deliver them to you with the guarantee of lower CPTs [costs per thousand] than terrestrial television'. This, it is claimed, eliminates any risk of advertising on a new medium and counters the inflationary spiral of current ITV rates. It will be possible to 'aim your TV advertising more precisely to reach elusive target audiences'. Each programme strand has its defined audience. Thus Sky Channel is described in its publicity material as a particularly efficient way of reaching the housewife and family audiences. Sky News will deliver 'a wide spread of audience types' who are 'sure to be watching closely'. A 'unique sponsorship packet' allows advertisers to be associated with this high-quality programme. Eurosport is aimed at what is admit- ted to be 'this elusive audience' and is 'a unique opportunity to catch the sports enthusiasts at their most attentive'. If Sky Movies can be sure of 'leadership in satellite television' it is primarily because it hopes to deliver specific audiences at a low price. Nor is Sky Television alone in having a policy of delivering a closely defined audience to the advertisers, as Bob Hunter of BSB makes clear.

> The audience for television consists of two things. There are people who watch loads of television. There are people who don't watch a load of television. Certain programmes attract larger groups of the difficult-to-get-at audience and we will be trying to get them because we can't deliver a very big audience. Our service isn't available to the 21 million homes in the UK from Day One. So it's important to have a targeted audience, and – if we have small numbers – that we can actually say: The people who are watching the programme during the day are women under the age of 35 – the people who are watching the entertainment programme at night are men and women under the age of 35 who are As, Bs, or ABs. So that we can deliver a targeted audience. That is done by looking at the sort of programmes that appeal to these people and a soap opera can cover a whole range of different target groups. We'll try and pick the one that targets our group.

The admission that audiences will be small – certainly at first – is one from which terrestrial broadcasters may draw some comfort. No doubt the audiences will grow, but people have only a finite amount of viewing time to split between terrestrial television, VCRs, satellite transmissions and perhaps cable. The Controller of BBC 2 draws comfort from this fact.

> The way the audience figures are worked out is such that even if you have access to Sky or BSB or other satellites the question will be how much of your time do you spend watching these channels. Say 30 per cent of the population spend 20 per cent of their time watching them, that fraction isn't as appalling as it might appear.

The logical consequence is – if one looks aside from specialist channels, e.g. sport or pop – that general programming by satellite will (as Gunnar Rugheimer admits) have to compete for audiences with the BBC and ITV.

We believe that only by providing programming of an equal quality to programming which is currently available on the existing channel will we have any hope that people will buy a BSB dish. Indeed to attract them we need to provide programming of higher quality or for groups of people who are not being catered for at the moment.

But there is concern among those people who might be expected to provide a proportion of that programming – the independents.

We are actively pursuing the satellite operators to find out whether their grandiloquent statements on how much they intend to spend on programming and their commitment to independent production will be met. We are very concerned in two ways.

One is that the price they are offering per hour [for programmes] is extremely low. It is a tenth of what terrestrial broadcasters are offering on average. And some of the sums are unimaginably low. We know of people trying to negotiate programmes for simple studio formats as low as £2,000 per hour. The effect of that is two-fold. They will become significant competitors from the mid-90s onward and will be active in the current market-place. They will therefore have an effect on our terrestrial partners, which will have an effect on their dealings with us.

Secondly, it raises the whole debate about what kind of television, texturally, qualitatively, we'll be looking at in the mid to late 90s.

The situation is complicated by the fact that not all pro-grammes will be specially commissioned. There are production companies and television organisations in the United States, in Japan and elsewhere which have produced and will continue to produce programmes which television channels, whether terrestrial or satellite, can acquire – some of them at very low prices. The satellite systems will, in Paul Styles's view, use a great deal of acquired programmes.

> Acquired programming is used in the schedule under the current terrestrial regime to fill your slots and leave you more money to spend on your originated programming. That is how it has worked to the advantage of both broadcaster and independent producer. Research shows that around the world the price of acquired material will rise dramatically when more people come into the market-place for it – it's just like any other goods or services.
>
> For example, since Berlusconi [the Italian TV magnate] has been actively buying American products for his three channels in Italy, the average price has tripled. It was $7,000 an hour at the beginning of 1987; it is now $23,000 per hour.

One of the things, Paul Styles explains, that happens when satellite operators compete for movie rights and sports rights is that they, as it were, squeeze money out of the system – money which either they or the terrestrial broadcasters might have spent on independent producers. In other words, competition for acquired programmes will force the price steadily upwards; this will force programme contractors, whether for terrestrial or satellite channels, to economise on specially commissioned programmes – programmes which the independents would expect to be asked to make. To meet the demand for pro-grammes which the proliferation of channels will bring about, the only answer, he concludes, will be bulk production, perhaps in the hands of independent producers but even more probably in the hands of bulk producers using factory methods.

> In the old days the large centralised studio complexes of the vertically integrated broadcasting systems supplied everything from beginning to end. The Eighties have seen the development of – if you like – off-shore operators, ourselves, who are able to do most of those

things outside of the broadcasting system and supply completed programmes for transmission . . . The outside edge of analysis shows that we'll be needing a quadrupling to a quintupling of the number of hours that we'll need to fill the screen – and it is not all going to be made in the ways we have programmes made now. So thinking elliptically, we go from the large box-factory producers inside the vertically integrated broadcasting organisations through the independent cycle back to a new kind of factory production system. If you look at the Sky facility that's being built in the West of London – the Osterley facility – it is basically being set up as a factory to produce programming cheaply – game shows, simple conversational format shows, that can be shot back-to-back 24 hours a day. That's the way they'll get their through-put which will be spiced with acquired movies and sports rights and bought-in material from around the world, including re-runs of terrestrial television formats. So we see for independent producers it is going to be a lean, tight bulk supply market.

The accusation that the satellite franchise-holders are not prepared to spend money on programmes is naturally strongly denied by those involved, like Gunnar Rugheimer of BSB.

It is quite clear that all this talk about a lot of slop to fill up the hours is nonsense. That wouldn't work at all. It is quite clear that you can produce programmes for a lot less money than the established broadcasters do . . . You can do it a lot cheaper without sacrificing quality. You can't do things below a certain level whatever happens – in terms of quality. But of course you can even out that cost by repeating good stuff and we are in a rather good situation because we will count on an exponential growth. Let's say ten people would be around to watch in Week 1 and a hundred and fifty might be around in Week 2 – so there's a repeat potential you can build into this and also get a higher degree of use out of the investment in production.

Comparisons between the £66,000 the BBC reputedly spends per hour on television programmes compared with what BSB is prepared to spend – namely £8,000 – are dismissed as invidious by the Managing Director of BSB.

> This is a pretty simplistic view because you don't have to spend £8,000 across the hour every hour – you don't have to spend it evenly at all. You can buy a lot of programming for a lot less and if you work out proper repeat schedules in the early years you are going to get a lot more mileage out of the pounds you have spent than that sort of straight-across-the-board figure would indicate.

But what of the suggestion that satellite broadcasting might acquire a reputation for re-runs when they ought to be showing new material? To which Gunnar Rugheimer's answer is that it will take time to build up an audience for satellites starting at perhaps 400,000 at the beginning of Year 1 and going to, say, 10 million in ten years' time. He continues:

> There's an inverse aspect of this which means this business of saying there are so many repeats does not necessarily have the same effect as it would if you ran a large number of repeats on the BBC, because there's the communality of experience involved in watching the BBC. The BBC is such a large universe that you'd very quickly get talked about if you were to do that.

Perhaps, he suggests, the real difficulty a new satellite channel faces is the introduction of the unfamiliar to its audience.

> I think in some ways you may arguably be better off as a programme philosophy to try to acquire programmes – whether they be British or foreign – with which people are already familiar. Because at least then the battle of acceptance doesn't have to be fought by you.

So clearly the policy of 'another chance to see' – the formula terrestrial broadcasters invented to describe repeats of old programmes – will be widely used on BSB.

> We can spend a large sum of money on programming and then be prepared to repeat that programme on a regular basis because we have a tiny and growing audience . . . Because we are a thematic channel and because we have so much air time we can give people another opportunity to see . . . Which means if we spend £100,000 on a programme and then show it over a six-months period half a dozen times it is actually quite a cheap programme for us.

It is a sound economic argument. But some might ask how a programme policy based on newish feature films and repeats is going to provide the kind of quality programming that will persuade viewers to make the capital outlay necessary to obtain the satellite signal and then to subscribe £10 a month to see the encrypted films. But BSB has confidence in subscription, which is breaking new ground by altering the way television is funded. This does not mean, says Bob Hunter of BSB, that advertising will be neglected.

> Advertising becomes easier as we get a larger base of people, a universe of homes, but it is always an important part of the mix and that's why we will target audiences who are important to advertisers and who are not being satisfied by television at the moment.

But it is subscription that Rugheimer sees as the 'locomotive'.

> The primary thing that would drive us to success we hope is the subscription business. Advertising is important and it could in time – when we're large and fat – we hope be even more important, but no one could take a satellite service up on advertising alone. Until you can deliver viewers in numbers you don't get very much advertising income anyway. The only way we can get to that point is by the subscription service.

It can, however, be argued that the British public has had

excellent television to date and has not had to pay for it. That this is a danger BSB acknowledges in its publicity in a curiously opaque statement, the logic of which is not easy to follow.

There is a natural reluctance on the part of consumers, used to thinking of television as 'free', to commit themselves to paying for it. But considering the amount of time the average Briton devotes to watching television – some 24 hours per week – the amount of money spent directly by each family is minimal. The success of video shows the willingness of a substantial proportion of viewers to opt for more choice – and to pay for it – despite the inconvenience of video rental.

The question is: What is satellite television going to offer the viewers that they might be willing to pay for? Gunnar Rugheimer has clear views on the subject.

Every study that has been made shows that people will pay for a feature film service. The terrestrial broadcasters do not have the quality of feature film or the newness of feature films we can offer. Murdoch will have his quota of exclusive films and we will have our quota of exclusive films but the terrestrial broadcasters will not have that. The free television window will come after the pay window and substantially after the pay window and there will be people who are prepared – large numbers of people if the price is right – who are prepared to pay for having a film service on tap.

But the situation in British television is not the same as in the United States where people welcomed the satellite channels because they offered something better than the American networks.

We come from a different base from America. America started with three networks, which are riddled with advertising at every possible moment and therefore for the audience to watch programmes which were not broken up in that way – on Home Box Office and so on – was a pleasant relief and a different way of watching

television; people needed that. Here I think the base is
different: you can watch, for instance, uncut movies on
television; we don't have things like the American
networks to escape from. Perhaps people want more choice
on television; it's not yet proven that they do but they
probably would be grateful for it. I don't think the BBC has
to worry about satellite television much for the next three
years maybe – who knows what it's going to be after that?
It's not at all clear whether Sky and BSB will survive. The
danger would be, I think, if they became very successful
and the BBC became more like PBS in America and
marginalised. That would be the end of the BBC as we
know it.

Meanwhile it looks like a duel in the sun using feature films.
BSB naturally thinks it will win in the shoot-out. There is
general agreement that in the long run there will be only one
survivor – Sky or BSB.

One organisation which might at one time have moved into
satellite broadcasting was the BBC; but it withdrew from the
adventure. If it sticks to its present policies it is not likely to
show interest in either of the available channels. It is the BBC
that was invited to take part in using one of the channels on the
UK satellite and found it an unhappy experience, as Bill Cotton,
who was involved in the negotiations, explains.

The BBC found itself in the middle of what was a
political argument between the Home Office who
regulate broadcasting and the Department of Trade and
Industry. There were enormous bureaucratic
restrictions. We were told we would have to broadcast to
a certain standard. We were told we would have to buy
our machinery from a consortium that was set up by the
DTI. Every which way we went we were regulated out of
existence. After I'd looked at it over a long period of
time and I'd tried to get something together it became
obvious to me that we were dealing with a government
who didn't understand the nature of broadcasting.
No doubt this experience reinforced the BBC's resolve as

expressed by its Director General to keep out of this branch of the business, especially in view of the new realism of their strategic thinking.

> One of the great changes we've made is to say the BBC doesn't have to be in everything that moves and breathes in British broadcasting. We have a role in broadcasting which is clearly based on public service, on the two television networks with their regional variations and on radio. We don't need to be bidding for satellite channels to do it. Now there will come a time when satellite might be the form of distribution which we require – for example, for high definition television. We want to be in high definition television and it may be that the most appropriate method to distribute it might be a satellite. That will in effect be just buying a transmitter in the sky rather than a transmitter on a hill.

The Director General goes on to say that in the meantime there is room and the willingness to collaborate with the satellite franchise-holders.

> We are acting in co-operation with satellite broadcasting. We are not taking the view of ITV that the best thing to do with satellite television is to shoot it down. What we are doing is cooperating with satellite broadcasting – for example in film deals, which means the satellite window is acquired by a satellite partner and the terrestrial rights are acquired by the BBC. That is helping us financially and it is giving the BBC viewer precisely the service he [sic] was used to getting with the same terrestrial window for us. We are cooperating with Sky and with BSB on that approach. We are cooperating on sports deals – with the Sky Bruno fight where our audience had access to the recording. Sky had the live event. We're cooperating on the FA Cup. We have a football deal with BSB. Again our general policy will be to cooperate with the satellite services where it is mutually advantageous to us and to our purposes. That is the basic attitude we are taking. We are not saying that we must go all out to try and destroy them.

Future Prospects

By the time this book appears the White Paper will have been translated into a long and complicated Broadcasting Bill which the Government must get through both Houses of Parliament in 1990 if the new Independent Television Commission is to be fully functioning by 1992 when the new commercial television franchises must be renewed.

The passing of the Bill will put an end to some of the speculation about the shape and future economy of British broadcasting; but there will still be some unresolved issues, chief of which must be the future of the BBC and its financing. Alan Yentob, Controller of BBC2, expresses the kind of anxiety which will remain until the next debate over the terms of the Charter takes place.

If the BBC has to compete for subscription service with all the other subscription channels – if that happened in this century – then I think there is no chance that you could provide the same service as you do at the moment. That's my belief. If you were to remove the licence fee and say Let them pay by subscription and those that want will take, I don't think you'll be able to raise the right sort of money. I don't think that the kind of democratisation of British broadcasting, which has at least existed for the last twenty years, i.e. that a lot of programmes, serious as well as entertainment programmes, are made available to a wide audience, will continue.

1989 saw the anniversary of the birth of John Reith, who first formulated the concept of public service broadcasting. The BBC is notoriously given to celebrating anniversaries. Opportunities should not be lacking to celebrate the positive side of the system he launched. It is remarkable that (at the time of writing) neither the Chairman nor the Director General of the BBC has created an opportunity – never a difficult task for a public figure – to speak out in defence of public service and the role it might have in a world so different from that in which Reith formulated the concept. One cannot imagine Reith remaining silent in similar circumstances. But then the Governors of the BBC have been remarkably reticent over episodes like the Zircon Affair and the censorship applied to the reporting of political utterance in Ulster. There have been no principled statements in defence of journalistic freedom and no resignations from the Board of Governors. One possible deduction is that they have no fundamental disagreement with the Government's policies on broadcasting. It may, of course, be merely that they have made a canny judgement and decided to keep their ammunition for the debate over the Charter, to avoid confrontations with the Government; but there is an argument which says that if the BBC does not speak up in defence of public service when ITV is under attack and being required to accept deregulation, then it is unlikely to find much support when the Corporation in turn comes under fire – as it will – in the Nineties when the BBC Charter will be renewed and rewritten. Ironically it has fallen to many who in the past were radical critics of public service institutions to defend the principle on which they are founded. Many of the criticisms are still valid. They refer to the way the institutions are governed and to the choice of people to discharge that function, to the relatively narrow spectrum of opinion that is given expression on the air, to the still limited interpretation of access. If they now find themselves defending the BBC (and the IBA) it is because they enshrine (however imperfectly) the ideal that broadcasting is more than a matter of economics – that it has a social and cultural dimension of great importance. The danger is, as Sir Richard Attenborough has said, that 'should all that is proposed in the White Paper come to pass, broadcasting in Britain will become a great deal *less* liberal rather than *more* liberal and plural'.

One of the main threats to the future of broadcasting as we have known it is thought by some to be satellite television. It is clearly going to be some time before we know how successful the new channels will be; they are at the time of writing encountering some initial difficulties. Sky, for instance, is very far behind its target for sales of dishes. It has lost its Disneyland channel, which was aimed at the family and children, and was a main selling point. BSB has problems with the production both of its 'squarial' and of an essential microchip and has had to postpone its first transmission to a vague date in 'the spring' of 1990. This long delay is bound to raise financial problems at a time when City institutions are reported to be sceptical about an enormously costly venture. Costs are reckoned to be £750 million for the first three years. But if these difficulties are overcome, satellite television received by DSB or distributed by cable will become a challenge to terrestrial television. The Secretary General of BETA takes a pessimistic view of the prospect.

It will have an immediate effect on ITV because if it survives it will take advertising money and therefore there will be less advertising for the present ITV channels. That means that ITV programming policy will be further eroded – and it is already being eroded. The satellite programmes – we know what they're going to be – they're going to be either cheaply done in this country or cheaply bought from abroad. And if ITV wants to survive it will have to go down-market with them . . .
The BBC will only survive if two things are guaranteed. One is the continuation of the licence fee system and the second is if there is some other element in broadcasting which has a public service content to it. If the BBC is the only protagonist of public service broadcasting and if the licence fee is under threat I think the BBC ultimately will die.

There is a contrary view from the commercial side of the industry, expressed by Charles Levison, Managing Director of Virgin Broadcasting, which plays down the impact which the established broadcasters will face from the changed circumstances.

> The major broadcasters in this country and in much of the other European countries are going to continue to get the majority of viewing and the majority of advertising revenue for a long period of time. Look at the American example where there is no major linguistic issue and where it has taken ten years for the three major networks to drop from 99 per cent to 62 per cent of the viewing.

The impact of satellites must, however, he believes, be looked at in a wider context of Europe and of satellite signals that transcend frontiers. It is a rich market waiting for exploitation.

> There is no doubt that there is a vast unutilised advertising revenue pool available for television all over northern Europe. The problem for the advertiser is in finding an outlet for his advertising money. Availability of television time is restricted in many ways. The problem for the transfrontier television station is in focusing that advertising revenue into purchasing budgets . . . The overall cake is several billion pounds.

BSB is more sceptical. According to its publicity, it believes that, for the foreseeable future, there will be no real pan-European television market.

> Language differences and lack of advertising support have led pan-European channels into low quality, lowest common denominator programming. BSB will conserve all its programme rights payments for its British audience and concentrate on serving its tastes.

Which would appear to be a nice combination of patriotism and economic hardheadedness.

This view is not shared by Super Channel which started in January 1987 and today claims 15 million homes in 15 countries as its potential audience. (The word 'potential' – as in all figures for satellite audiences – is important.) Super Channel faces two problems, however: how to deal with linguistic barriers and how rapidly transfrontier budgets will expand. Charles Levison of Virgin Productions explains how the cultural linguistic issue is tackled.

> First by choice of programmes – music and sport are both highly international – you don't need to understand much of the language. Also the type of music that is enjoyed – particularly by younger people – in Germany is very similar to that in the UK or Finland or Brussels. The same is true of sport. More difficult areas are news and particularly drama. Documentaries can be very visual, and therefore language is not such a great issue.

Satellite signals, he continues, are frequently distributed to viewers by cable systems, which allows technical equipment to be introduced at cable distribution points 'to enable you to show Dutch subtitles in Dutch cable systems but not to show Dutch subtitles in German cable systems. All of that is now available'.

As for the budgets, they are said to be expanding rapidly.

> The question is whether they will expand fast enough to deal with the level of costs that Super Channel require to run a general entertainment television channel that crosses frontiers. It can't be done for less than £10 million a year – that's absolute rock bottom.

It is a figure to put alongside the figure for BBC2, which in the year 1986/87 was a global £150 million.

There are other problems facing pan-European television. Paul Bainsfair of Saatchi & Saatchi cites local codes governing advertising.

> There are some places where you can advertise cigarettes still – on television in Greece, I think – and it is virtually impossible to advertise cigarettes in any kind of an active way in the UK and there are other markets in Europe where you can't market cigarettes. So there are product types where you have a problem. There are other

product types which can be advertised but because of the rules – governing alcohol, for example, or products to do with sensitive areas like sanitary protection – where you'll find that there are quite big differences. When that happens you have to guard against writing advertising to the lowest common denominator. In other words, if there's one market-place in Europe where you can only do so much, you don't then run that advertising in markets where you can do a great deal more. So you have to accept that you can't achieve the kind of harmony of advertising message we would like.

There are, moreover, cultural differences to be taken into account because, although there are many products available right across Europe in exactly the same format in terms of packaging and branding, yet the customers are not culturally uniform. John Blakemore of Ogilvy & Mather explains the problem.

They take different things out of products. They look for different things. For example, the toothpaste market in the UK – it is very much centred around people. They look upon toothpaste as something that is good for you. It's for healthy gums. It's to stop children's teeth decaying. It's to stop their teeth falling out. If you go to the rest of Europe that's not the important element. The important element is just to have gleaming teeth. It's more of a beauty aid. And obviously if you have one commercial that is aimed at saying 'This toothpaste is good for you – it stops the build-up of tartar' that would work in the UK but it might not work in other countries. So I think you have to be careful about transfrontier television. It won't always work. It will for some brands. Coca-Cola is the perfect example most people would quote. Products like Levi jeans – because their positioning is the same in almost every market in the world. And generally these products are aimed at the youth market. But I would say that 80 per cent of advertising will still be aimed at a local market, i.e. a UK market, a French market, or a Spanish market.

How European satellite broadcasting develops will depend on the way in which Europe develops politically and economically and what part Britain plays in the new situation after 1992. If Europe develops as a force of very considerable economic and political power, as a new element in the pattern of world politics, then it will constitute a rich market which the advertisers will be eager to enter. The young generation mentioned above will become a middle-aged one, many of them at home in the lingua franca of the modern world – English. Through satellite transmissions powerful financial groups will reach out to that market, screening not only advertisements which are understood across frontiers but programmes which are constructed to appeal internationally. Since the main interests of the advertisers are financial and not cultural and since many of the agencies involved will be US-based, the cultural–political problem is already causing concern, as David Glencross of the IBA explains.

> What we would prefer to see – and what indeed all governments in Western Europe are working towards – is some kind of general international agreement on the broad regulation of transcountry broadcasting – satellite broadcasting essentially. There are discussions going on both within the European Community and also within the Council of Europe (the Council covers more states than the Community) for a convention . . . on the amount of advertising and on at least statements of principle to encourage European production and to make sure that satellite television and cross-country broadcasting is not wholly dominated by acquired material principally from America.

Behind European concern lies the question of what will become of national and local cultures. To what extent are they worth defending? To what extent is the cultural question a stalking horse for reactionary political attitudes? Why – to put it crudely – is it all right to import Henry James, Truman Capote,

Edith Wharton, Salinger, Arthur Miller and the Hollywood greats and not American soap operas? These are questions immensely complicated by the inevitable entry into Europe of large populations whose cultural traditions are different from, but not less valuable than, the autochthonous ones – Turks, Indians, Pakistanis, Chinese, Arabs, Afro-Caribbean people, Vietnamese. Perhaps it will be the role of terrestrial television – along with national and local radio services – to reflect the variety of ways of life, the languages, traditions and ethnic cultures which the Europe of the future will contain and to encourage understanding and tolerance among the cultural groups. That will be a public service – one likely to be undertaken only by broadcasting institutions dedicated to that concept and so funded that they can discharge that cultural and political task.

List of Contributors

Paul Bainsfair, Managing Director, Saatchi & Saatchi
John Blakemore, Media Head of Broadcast Buying, Ogilvy
   & Mather
Melvyn Bragg, Head of Arts, London Weekend Television
Michael Checkland, Director General, BBC
Bill Cotton, formerly Managing Director, BBC Television
Jon Davey, Director General, Cable Authority
David Elstein, Director of Programmes, Thames Television
Liz Forgan, Director of Programmes, Channel 4 Television
David Glencross, Director of Television, IBA
Michael Grade, Chief Executive, Channel 4 Television
Tony Hearn, Secretary General, BETA
Bob Hunter, Managing Director of Now and Galaxy
   Channels, BSB
Charles Levison, Managing Director, Virgin Broadcasting
Kenneth Miles, Director, Incorporated Society of British
   Advertisers
David Nicholas, Chairman, ITN
David Plowright, Chairman, Broadcasting Division, Granada
   Television
Jonathan Powell, Controller, BBC1
Lord Rees-Mogg, Chairman, Broadcasting Standards Council
David Rose, Head of Drama, Channel 4 Television
Gunnar Rugheimer, Director of Corporate Development,
   BSB
George Russell, Chairman, IBA
Alan Sapper, General Secretary, ACTT
Mark Shivas, Head of Drama Group, BBC Television
Janet Street-Porter, Head of Youth Programming, BBC TV
Paul Styles, Director, Independent Programme Producers
   Association

Brian Tesler, Chairman and Managing Director, London
  Weekend Television
Sir Ian Trethowan, Chairman, Thames Television
David Wheeler, Director General, Institute of Practitioners in
  Advertising
Frank Willis, Controller of Advertising, IBA
Alan Yentob, Controller, BBC2

Index

A figure 2 in brackets after a page reference means that the subject is referred to under two different headings on the page.